Jim —
In The spirit of '76,
Love The world and
be free!
Jim
Dec. 7, 2015

OUR ONLY WORLD

OUR ONLY WORLD

TEN ESSAYS

Wendell Berry

COUNTERPOINT

BERKELEY

The author thanks the editors of the following magazines in which several of these essays first were published: *Farming*, *The Progressive*, *The Christian Century*, *Harper's*, and *The Atlantic* (online).

Library of Congress Cataloging-in-Publication Data is available.
ISBN 978-1-61902-488-5

Cover design by Emma Cofod
Interior Design by David Bullen

COUNTERPOINT
2560 Ninth Street, Suite 318
Berkeley, CA 94710
www.counterpointpress.com

Printed in the United States of America
Distributed by Publishers Group West

10 9 8 7 6 5 4 3 2 1

I dedicate this book to the following good companions
who honored our state's capitol by their presence
and me by their kindness:

Lisa Abbott
Chad Berry
Teri Blanton
Doug Doerrfeld
Brandon Goodwin
Rick Handshoe
John Hennen
Silas House
Jason Howard
Beverly May
Mickey McCoy
Martin Mudd
Matt Murray
Kevin Pentz
Herb E. Smith
Lora Smith
Stanley Sturgill
Tanya Turner
Patty Wallace

Contents

1. Paragraphs from a Notebook   *3*

2. The Commerce of Violence   *15*

3. A Forest Conversation   *21*

4. Local Economies to Save the Land and the People   *53*

5. Less Energy, More Life   *69*

6. Caught in the Middle   *73*

7. On Receiving One of the Dayton
Literary Peace Prizes   *97*

8. Our Deserted Country   *105*

9. For the 50-Year Farm Bill   *159*

10. On Being Asked for "A Narrative for the Future"   *167*

Acknowledgments   *177*

OUR ONLY WORLD

TEN ESSAYS

I

Paragraphs from a Notebook

[2010]

WE NEED TO acknowledge the formlessness inherent in the analytic science that divides creatures into organs, cells, and ever smaller parts or particles according to its technological capacities.

I recognize the possibility and existence of this knowledge, even its usefulness, but I also recognize the narrowness of its usefulness and the damage it does. I can see that in a sense it is true, but also that its truth is small and far from complete.

———————

In and by all my thoughts and acts, I am opposed to any claim that such knowledge is adequate to the sustenance of human life or the health of the ecosphere.

Do even the professionals and experts believe in it, in the sense of acting on it in their daily lives? I doubt that they do.

To this science, the body is an assembly of parts provisionally joined, a "basket case" sure enough. A mountain is a heap of "resources" unfortunately mixed with substances that are not marketable.

There is an always significant difference between knowing and believing. We may know that the earth turns, but we believe, as we say, that the sun rises. We know by evidence, or by trust in people who have examined the evidence in a way that we trust is trustworthy. We may sometimes be persuaded to believe by reason, but within the welter of our experience reason is limited and weak. We believe always by coming, in some sense, to see. We believe in what is apparent, in what we can imagine or "picture" in our minds, in what we feel to be true, in what our hearts tell us, in experience, in stories—above all, perhaps, in stories.

We can, to be sure, see parts and so believe in them. But there has always been a higher seeing that informs us that parts, in themselves, are of no worth. Genesis is right: "It is not good that the man should be alone." The phrase "be alone" is a contradiction in terms. A brain alone is a dead brain. A man alone is a dead man.

We are thus as likely to be wrong in what we know as in what we believe.

We may know, or think we know, and often say, that humans are "only" animals, but we teach our children specifically human virtues—evidently because we believe that they are not "only" animals.

Another question of knowledge and belief that keeps returning to my mind is this: Are there not some things that cannot be known apart from belief? This question refers not just to matters of religion—as in Job 19:25: "I know that my redeemer liveth, and that he shall stand at the latter day upon the earth ..." —but also to ordinary motives of family and community life such as love, compassion, and forgiveness. Do people who believe that such motives are genetically determined have the same knowledge as people who believe that they are the results of choice, culture, cultivation, and discipline? Or: Do people who believe in the sanctity or intrinsic worth of the world and its creatures have the same knowledge as people who recognize only market value? If there is no way to measure or prove such differences of knowledge, that does at least prove one of my points: There is more to us than some of us suppose.

We may know the anatomy of the body to the extent of the anatomy of atoms, and yet we love and instruct our children as whole persons. And we accept an obligation to help them to preserve their wholeness, which is to say their health. This is not an obligation that we can safely transfer to the subdivided and anatomizing medical industry, not even for the sake of cures. Cures, to industrial medicine, are marketable products extractable from bodies. To cure in this sense is not to heal. To heal is to make whole, not so ideologically definable or so technologically possible or so handily billable.

This applies as well to the industries of landscapes: agriculture, forestry, and mining. Once they have been industrialized, these enterprises no longer recognize landscapes as *wholes*, let alone as the homes of people and other creatures. They regard landscapes as sources of extractable products. They have "efficiently" shed any other interest or concern.

We have come to this by way of the disembodiment of thought—a mentalization, almost a puritanization, of thought—depriving us of the physical basis of a sympathy that might join us kindly to landscapes and their creatures, including their human creatures. This purity or sublimity of thought is hard to account for, for it has come about under the sponsorship of materialism. Perhaps it happened because materialists, instead of assigning ultimate value to materiality as would have been reasonable, have abstracted "material" to "mechanical," and thus have removed from it all bodily or creaturely attributes. Or perhaps the abstracting impulse branched in either of two directions: one toward the mechanical, the other toward the financial, which is to say toward the so-called economy of money as opposed to the actual economy (oikonomia or "house-keeping") of goods. Either way the result is the same: the scientific-industrial culture, founded nominally upon materialism, arrives at a sort of fundamentalist disdain for material reality. The living world is then treated as dead matter, the worth of which is determined exclusively by the market.

This highly credentialed, highly politicized disdain, now allied with the similar disdain of highly spiritualized religions, is limitlessly destructive. We cannot say that its destructiveness has been unnoticed as it has been happening, or that the dissolutions, and the dissoluteness, of mechanical thought have not been, by some, well understood. The poet William Butler Yeats prayed: "God guard me from the thoughts men think / In the mind alone . . ." ("A Prayer for Old Age"). He wrote in 1916: "We only believe in those thoughts which have been conceived not in the brain but in the whole body"

(Introduction to *Certain Noble Plays of Japan*, by Ezra Pound and Ernest Fenollosa). In the same essay he spoke with foreboding of "a mechanical sequence of ideas."

As another example, more explicit, here is the critic and translator Philip Sherrard on the Greek poet Anghelos Sikelianos: "He saw [the western world of his time] as increasingly alienated from those principles which give life significance and beauty and as approaching the condition of a machine out of control and hastening towards destruction. . . . The organic sense of life was being shattered into countless unconnected fragments. . . . A system of learning which made extreme demands on the purely mechanical and sterile processes of memory had the effect of absorbing all the spontaneous movements of body and soul of the younger generations" (*The Wound of Greece*, 72, 74).

Or here is a passage, by the poet and critic John Crowe Ransom, pointed more directly at our specialist system, which he identified as a phase of the Puritanism that began in religion: "You may dissociate the elements of experience and exploit them separately. But then at the best you go on a schedule of small experiences, taking them in turn, and trusting that when the rotation is complete you will have missed nothing. And at the worst you will become so absorbed in some one small experience that you will forget to go on and complete the schedule; in that case you will have missed something.

The theory that excellence lies in the perfection of the single functions, and that society should demand that its members be hard specialists, assumes that there is no particular harm in missing something (*The World's Body*, 71).

A proper attention to our language, moreover, informs us that the Greek root of "anatomy" means "dissection," and that of "analysis" means "to undo." The two words have essentially the same meaning. Neither suggests a respect for formal integrity. I suppose that the nearest antonym to both is a word we borrow directly from Greek: *poiesis*, making or creation, which suggests that the work of the poet, the composer or maker, is the necessary opposite to that of the analyst and the anatomist. Some scientists, I think, are in this sense poets.

But we appear to be deficient in learning or teaching a competent concern for the way that parts are joined. We certainly are not learning or teaching adequately the arts of forming parts into wholes, or the arts of preserving the formal integrity of the things we receive as wholes already formed.

Without this concern and these arts, our efforts of conservation are probably futile. Without some sense of necessary connections and a competent awareness of human and natural limits, the issues of scale and form are not only pointless, but cannot even enter our consciousness.

My premise is that there is a scale of work at which our minds are as effective and even as harmless as they ought to be, at which we can be fully responsible for consequences and there are no catastrophic surprises. But such a possibility does not excite us.

What excites us is some sort of technological revolution: the fossil fuel revolution, the automotive revolution, the assembly line revolution, the antibiotic revolution, the sexual revolution, the computer revolution, the "green revolution," the genomic revolution, and so on. But these revolutions—all with something to sell that people or their government "must" buy—are mere episodes of the one truly revolutionary revolution perhaps in the history of the human race: the Industrial Revolution, which has proceeded from the beginning with only two purposes: to replace human workers with machines, and to market its products, regardless of their usefulness or their effects, at the highest possible profit—and so to concentrate wealth into ever fewer hands.

This revolution has, so far, fulfilled its purposes, with remarkably few checks or thwarts. I say "so far" because its great weakness obviously is its dependence on what it calls "natural resources," which it has used ignorantly and foolishly, and which it has progressively destroyed. Its weakness, in short, is that its days are numbered. Having squandered nature's "resources," it will finally yield to nature's correction, which in prospect grows ever harsher.

We have formed our present life, including our economic and intellectual life upon specialization, professionalism, and competition. Certified smart people expect to solve all problems by analysis, dividing wholes into ever smaller parts. Science and industry do give room to synthesis, but by that they do not mean putting back together the things once together that they have taken apart; they mean making something "synthetic." They mean engineering the disassembled parts, by some manner of violence, into profitable new commodities. In such a state of things we don't see or, apparently, suspect the complexity of connections among ecology, agriculture, food, health, and medicine (if by "medicine" we mean healing). Nor can we see how this complexity is necessarily contained within, and at the mercy of, human culture, which in turn is necessarily contained within the not very expandable limits of human knowledge and human intelligence.

We have accumulated a massive collection of "information" to which we may have "access." But this information, by being accessible, does not become knowledge. We might find, if such a computation were possible, that the amount of human knowledge over many millennia has remained more or less constant—that is it has always filled the available mental capacity—and therefore that learning invariably involves forgetting. To have the Renaissance, we had to forget the Middle Ages. To the extent that we have learned about machines, we have forgotten about plants and animals. Every nail we drive in, as I believe C. S. Lewis said, drives another out.

The thing most overlooked by scientists, and by the enviers and emulators of science in the humanities, is the complicity of science in the Industrial Revolution, which science has served not by supplying the "scientific" checks of skepticism, doubt, criticism, and correction, but by developing of marketable products, from refined fuels to nuclear bombs to computers to poisons to pills.

It has been remarkable how often science has hired out to the ready-made markets of depravity, as when it has served the military-industrial complex, which is solidly founded upon the hopeless logic of revenge, or the medical and pharmaceutical industries, which are based somewhat on the relief of suffering but also on greed, on the vicious circles of hypochondria, and on the inducible fear of suffering yet to come. The commodification of genome-reading rides upon the same fears of the future that palmistry and phrenology rode upon.

We may say with some confidence that the most apparently beneficent products of science and industry should be held in suspicion if they are costly to consumers or bring power to governments or profits to corporations.

There are, we know, scientists who are properly scrupulous, responsible, and critical, who call attention to the dangers of oversold and under-tested products, and who are almost customarily ignored. They are often called "independent scientists," and the adjective is significant, for it implies not only certain moral virtues but also political weakness. The combination of expertise, prestige, wealth, and power, incapable of self-doubt or self-criticism, is hardly to be deterred by a few "independent scientists."

Scientists in general, like humanists and artists in general, have accepted the industrialists' habit, or principle, of ignoring the contexts of life, of place, of community, and even of economy.

The capitalization of fear, weakness, ignorance, bloodthirst, and disease is certainly financial, but it is not, properly speaking, economic.

Criticism of scientific-industrial "progress" need not be balked by the question of how we would like to do without anesthetics or immunizations or antibiotics. Of course there have been benefits. Of course there have been advantages—at least to the advantaged. But valid criticism does not deal in categorical approvals and condemnations. Valid criticism attempts a just description of our condition. It weighs advantages against disadvantages, gains against losses, using standards more general and reliable than corporate profit or economic growth. If criticism involves computation, then it aims at a full accounting and an honest net result, whether a net gain or a net loss. If we are to hope to live sensibly, correcting mistakes that need correcting, we need a valid general criticism.

Scared for health, afraid of death, bored, dissatisfied, vengeful, greedy, ignorant, and gullible—these are the qualities of the ideal consumer. Can we imagine a way of education that would turn passive consumers into active and informed critics, capable of using their own minds in their own defense? It will not be the purely technical education-for-employment now advocated by the most influential "educators" and "leaders."

We have good technical or specialized criticism: A given thing is either a good specimen of its kind or it is not. A valid *general* criticism would measure work against its context. The health of the context—the body, the community, the ecosystem—would reveal the health of the work.

2

The Commerce
of Violence

[2013]

On the day of the bombing in Boston, *The New York Times* printed an op-ed piece by a human being who had been imprisoned at Guantanamo for more than eleven years, uncharged and of course untried. The occurrence of these two events on the same day was a coincidence, but that does not mean that they are unrelated.

What connects them is our devaluation, and when convenient our disvaluation, of human life as well as the earthly life of which human life is a dependent part. This cheapening of life, and the violence that inevitably accompanies it, is surely the dominant theme of our time. The ease and quickness with which we resort to violence would be astounding if it were not conventional.

In the Appalachian coal fields we mine coal by destroying a mountain, its forest, its waterways, and its human community without counting the destruction as a cost. Our military technicians, our representatives, sit in armchairs and kill our enemies, and our enemies' children, by remote control. In the Guantanamo prison, guards force their fasting prisoners to live, and they do so as routinely as in other circumstances they would kill them.

And the Boston bombing? Like most people, I was not there and I don't know anybody who was, but I was grieved and frightened by the news. This fearful grief has grown familiar to me since I first felt it at the start of World War II, but at each of its returns it is worse. Each new resort to violence enlarges the argument against our species, and the task of hope becomes harder.

I am absolutely in sympathy with those who suffered the bombing in Boston and with their loved ones. They have been singled out by a violence that was general in its intent, not aimed particularly at anybody. The oddity, the mystery, of a particular hurt from a general violence — the necessity to ask, "Why me? Why my loved ones?"—must compound the suffering. What I am less and less in sympathy with is the rhetoric and the tone of official indignation. Public officials cry out for justice against the perpetrators. I too wish them caught and punished. But I am unwilling to have my wish spoken for me in a tone of surprise and outraged innocence. The event in Boston is not unique or rare or surprising or in any way new. It is only another transaction in the commerce of violence: the unending, the not foreseeably endable, exchange of an eye for an eye, with customary justifications on every side, in which we fully participate; and beyond that, it is our willingness to destroy anything, any place, or anybody standing between us and whatever we are "manifestly destined" to have.

We congratulate ourselves perpetually upon our Civil War by which the slaves were, in a manner of speaking, "freed." We forget, if we have ever learned, that the same army that "freed the slaves" established for us the "right" of military violence against a civilian population, and then acted upon that "right" by a war of extermination against the native people of the West. Nobody who knows our history, from the "Indian wars" to our contemporary foreign wars of "homeland defense," should find anything unusual in the massacre of civilians and their children.

It is not possible for us to reduce the value of life, including human life, to nothing *only* to suit our own convenience or our own perceived need. By making this reduction for ourselves, we make it for everybody and anybody, even for our enemies, even for the maniacs whose enemies are schoolchildren or spectators at a marathon.

We forget also that violence is so securely founded among

us—in war, in forms of land use, in various methods of economic "growth" and "development"—because it is immensely profitable. People do not become wealthy by treating one another or the world kindly and with respect. Do we not need to remember this? Do we have a single eminent leader who would dare to remind us?

On the second day after the catastrophe in Boston, Thomas L. Friedman announced in the *Times* that "the right reaction is: Wash the sidewalk, wipe away the blood, and let whoever did it know that . . . they have left no trace on our society or way of life." We should, said Mr. Friedman, "let there be no reminder whatsoever." And he asserted, with a shocking indifference to evidence and his own language, that "the benefits—living in an open society—always outweigh the costs." He is speaking to (among others) people whose loved ones have been killed and people who will never again stand on their own legs. How can he think that all the traces of any violence can be easily wiped away? How would he wipe away the traces of a bombed village or a strip mine or a gullied field or a wrecked forest? The dead in Boston no longer live in an open society. How have *they* benefitted?

Mr. Friedman, like other journalists, asks us, as he wrote, to "notice how many people came *running toward the blast* within seconds to help." And that is very well. To know that people would run to help, perhaps at the risk of their lives, is consoling and reassuring. But we have got to acknowledge that the help that comes after the violence has been done, though it undeniably helps, is not a solution to violence.

The solution, many times more complex and difficult, would be to go beyond our ideas, obviously insane, of war as the way to peace and of permanent damage to the ecosphere as the way to wealth. Actually to help our suffering of one man-made horror after another, we would have to revise radically our understanding of economic life, of community life, of work, and of pleasure. We employ thousands of scientists and spend billions of dollars to reduce matter to its smallest particles and to search for farther stars. How many scientists and how many dollars are devoted to harmony between economy and ecology, or to amity and lenity in the face of hatred and killing?

To learn to meet our needs without continuous violence against one another and our only world would require an immense intellectual and practical effort, requiring the help of every human being perhaps to the end of human time.

This would be work worthy of the name "human." It would be fascinating and lovely.

3

A Forest
Conversation

[2012]

An ECOSYSTEM, the web of relationships by which
a place and its creatures sustain a mutual life, ultimately is
mysterious, like life itself. We can know enough, and probably only enough, to tell us how little we know and to make
us careful. At present, too ignorant to know how ignorant
we are, we believe that we are free to impose our will upon
the land with the utmost power and speed to gain the largest
profit in the shortest time, and we believe that there are no
penalties for this.

Industrial farming and forestry use extreme methodologies that barter the long-term health and fertility, which is to say the long-term productivity, of local ecosystems for a short-term monetary gain. Like mining, they tend, though not so suddenly, toward the same totality of ruin. The issue of land *use* is not on the agenda of most conservation organizations, which have been primarily concerned throughout their history with the preservation of wilderness and wildlife habitat, even though most land is being used, and used badly, and though no wilderness or wildlife can survive the prolonged abuse of the economic landscapes. Governments typically are preoccupied with the politics and commerce related to land use rather than the ever more pressing issues of land use itself: soil erosion, toxicity, ecological degradation, the destruction of rural communities, and the substitution of the global consumer culture for local cultures of husbandry. The considerable force of the colleges of agriculture has been applied mostly to promotion of industrial technologies and the economics of agribusiness, ignoring the great teachers and advocates of good land use: Liberty Hyde Bailey, J. Russell Smith, Hugh Hammond Bennett, Albert Howard, Aldo Leopold, and others. So utterly dominant has industrial agriculture become that the officially recommended soil conservation technology, "no-till agriculture," undertakes to "save" the soil by poisoning it. By this method, the noncommercial plant cover is killed with an herbicide, and then the "undisturbed" soil is planted in corn or soybeans genetically engineered for "herbicide resistance." Among the results of continuous no-till cropping on sloping land is severe soil erosion. Everything human and natural is sacrificed for the sake of annual production.

On the mostly wooded valley sides where I live, near the lower end of the Kentucky River, the same bad trade is under way. The woodlands here, which for the last three quarters of a century or so have enjoyed the flimsy beneficence of neglect, are now often as heartlessly cropped as the fields.

The story of a bad job of logging is easy to imagine. "We need money," a forest-owning family decides. "We'll sell our trees." "The environment" being in fashion, the family takes comfort in the thought that after the marketable trees are gone, many smaller trees will remain as the "next crop." And so they sell their "standing timber" to a logging company, whose representative comes in and marks every tree that can be sold.

And then, all too often, a sawyer and a driver of a mechanical skidder, employees of the logging company, arrive with, inevitably, the single purpose of cutting and removing the marked trees as quickly, which is to say as cheaply, as possible. The logging company is in every sense an absentee, and of all the short-term economies in forestry, the absentee logging company's is the shortest. Any concern for the "next crop" cherished by the owners, who also have in effect made themselves absentees, has become forceless. Standing trees, if they are unmarked, are now regarded merely as obstacles. There is little concern for directional felling. Many of the smaller trees are broken off or permanently bent or in other ways damaged by the marked trees as they fall. As the tree-length logs are dragged out of the woods, sometimes straight up or down a steep slope, the trees of the "next crop" are damaged by the skidder or by the dragged logs.

The woods is left a shambles, for nobody thought of the forest rather than the trees. All along the way, the economic interest was shifted from the forest to the marketable "standing timber," though the *source* of the timber is not the trees but the forest. Finally there is no significant difference between forest ecology and a long-term forest economy. To forget this profound kinship is to abandon the forest to bad work.

The example I have given is a worst case scenario, but my point is that when land abuse is normal and not a public issue, and when local land economies have disappeared into a global financial system, the worst case can happen easily. I asked William Martin, a forest ecologist living in Lexington, "What percentage of Kentucky's forest is sustainably managed?" He replied, "I would say less than ten." Jim Finley, a forester at Penn State, would apply the same fraction to the forest of Pennsylvania, but he suggests that "healthy" is a better term than "sustainably managed."

The damage extends to the human community when, as often happens, the cut timber is transported out of the neighborhood and even out of the state without so much as a stop at a sawmill, thus yielding the least possible local benefit from a local resource.

The U. S. Department of Agriculture and the land grant colleges of agriculture seem to regard forestry as a kind, or division, of farming. This risks confusion and requires thought. For example, the use of "harvesting" as a synonym for "logging" seems at first to be merely euphemistic; people of delicacy wish to have their woodlands "harvested" as they wish to have their meat "processed." But "harvest" (Middle English *hervest*, meaning "autumn") was associated originally with annual grain crops that ripen in the fall. When we harvest a crop of corn, we take all that is of economic worth—which, with some special exceptions, is a bad way to treat a forest.

Like the grasses and forbs of farm pastures and hayfields, trees are perennials. But *unlike* the grasses and forbs, which mature and can be cut once, or more than once, every year, trees keep growing bigger year after year, sometimes for hundreds of years. Forests also are more complex in structure and diversity of species. You can't learn to manage a forest by managing a pasture.

Farming, moreover, must always be to some extent a compromise with the local ecosystem. Whereas the farmer requires from the farm, specifically for human use, several plants and animals that the ecosystem in its natural state would not produce, the best foresters ask the local forest ecosystem only to continue to produce what, according to its nature, it produces best: primarily trees of the native species. A properly diversified forest economy produces more than trees, of course. And a healthy forest contributes to the health of the soil, water, air, and all other constituents of the natural world. The forest submits to compromise only by allowing the foresters to take timber and other forest products for human use, if they can do so without destroying the integrity and the continuous productivity of the ecosystem.

Forest owners, however, may have a good deal to learn from livestock farmers—little as such farmers may know about forestry. No sane farmer would sell all her brood cows, keep their heifer calves, and wait for another calf crop until the heifers have become old enough to breed and calve. But forest owners do substantially that when they sell off every marketable tree—except that the forest owners (or their descendants) may have to wait for generations, not years, for another marketable "crop."

Nor would a sane cattle farmer "highgrade" his herd by selling his best cows and keeping and breeding the worst. But people who highgrade their woodlands do exactly the same thing, selling the best and keeping the worst—which, if not thoughtless, as it usually is, would be insane.

The best logging, however, we may rightly call culling. The foresters' name for it is "worst-first single tree selection." By this method, the trees in the area to be logged are looked at individually, evaluated according to standards of worth and health, and the worst are carefully removed, leaving only small openings in the canopy, and doing the least possible damage to the trees, young and old, that remain, and to the forest floor. The "worst" are trees that are diseased or dying, leaning trees that are more likely to fall as they grow more top-heavy, trees that branch too low or are otherwise inferior in conformation.

But I need to interrupt myself here to notice that my need to be clear has led me into oversimplification. A stand consisting only of the "best" trees would be a tree farm, not a forest. A healthy forest would necessarily include some less valuable or unmarketable species and some diseased and dying trees, so as to sustain the finally unimaginable diversity of creatures that belong to the natural forest. Good foresters know this and are charitable toward members of the forest community that by the standards merely of economics would be considered worthless.

The essential point is that by applying the standard of ecological health, which is the standard of long-term economy, the good forester will leave standing numerous marketable trees because they are healthy and flourishing, and by doing so will maintain the forest at its highest productivity. The explanation for this comes from elementary geometry: A quarter inch of annual growth on a tree two feet in diameter is far more than a quarter inch of annual growth on a tree six inches in diameter. A flourishing large tree makes more marketable wood per year than many small ones. A woodland logged in this way can be logged fairly frequently, at intervals of ten or fifteen or twenty years. And at each successive logging the quality and marketability of the trees that are cut will have increased.

Forestry of this kind, though it is still far too rare, is not new. That it is more than four hundred years old we know from Aldo Leopold's essay, "The Last Stand," in *The River of the Mother of God*:

> I know a hardwood forest called the Spessart, covering a mountain on the north flank of the Alps. Half of it has sustained cuttings since 1605, but was never slashed. The other half was slashed during the 1600s, but has been under intensive forestry during the last 150 years. Despite this rigid protection, the old slashing now produces only mediocre pine, while the unslashed portion grows the finest cabinet oak in the world; one of those oaks fetches a higher price than a whole acre of the old slashings. On the old slashings the litter accumulates without rotting, stumps and limbs disappear slowly, natural reproduction is slow. On the unslashed portion litter disappears as it falls, stumps and limbs rot at once, natural reproduction is automatic. Foresters attribute the inferior performance of the old slashing to its depleted microflora, meaning that underground community of bacteria, molds, fungi, insects, and burrowing mammals which constitute half the environment of a tree (pp. 292–93).

By "slashed" Leopold evidently meant something like what we now mean by "clear-cut." "Slashing" destroyed the integrity of the forest ecosystem.

The literature on what we are now calling "sustainable agriculture," laying out the ecological principles of good land use, is fairly substantial, but not nearly so much has been written on sustainable forestry. To learn about that, it is necessary to become familiar with one or more of the few exemplary forests where good practice is well established and for which there is some published accounting, or one may study the ways and the work of exemplary loggers and forest managers. Bad logging, like bad farming, comes from estrangement between the industrial economy and nature's ecosystems. Most land users, as they come more and more to adopt industrial technologies and attitudes, know nothing or think nothing of ecology. And few ecologists or people oriented to ecology are involved with, or familiar with or even interested in, the economies of land use. When you find a farmer or a forester who has united the inescapable economic concern with an equally compelling interest in ecology, that is when you had better stop and take notice.

I first met Jason Rutledge a good many years ago when both of us were visiting Washington and Lee University in Lexington, Virginia, which is in Jason's home country. He was talking then, and he is talking still, on the closely related themes of sustainable forestry and logging with horses. Since that first encounter, our paths have crossed fairly often in the woods and at various field days and conferences. "Worst-first single tree selection" is language I first heard from Jason, a logger who uses horses (*Suffolk* horses, he would want me to say) to skid the logs out of the woods. He is also a teacher whose alumni are scattered about in the woods, horse logging on their own and earning a living by doing so.

It was Jason Rutledge who introduced me to Troy Firth. Like Jason, Troy is an advocate for sustainable forestry and is worth listening to because his advocacy, like Jason's, rests upon practice. Troy is a forest owner whose holdings are extensive. He is a forester and logger who operates his own sawmill. He is also owner and manager of Firth Maple Products, the chief product of which is maple syrup. This year Troy and his crew tapped 17,000 sugar maple trees and made 6,100 gallons of syrup. Next year they plan to tap 22,000 trees.

Troy has lived and worked all his life in the neighborhood near Spartansburg, Pennsylvania, long occupied by his family; his house is on Firth Road. Troy's involvement in the woodland economy of his region is elaborate and of long standing. He is not a waster of words, and I think this is because he is confident both of his knowledge and of the limits of his knowledge. He has a reliable sense of humor and is generous with his knowledge, but he generally keeps quiet until he has something worthwhile to say. The result is that when he talks you listen, and you are apt to be surprised at how much you remember of what he has said.

From his student days, Troy has been inclined toward the woods. While he was in college he took two years off to work as a logger. He accumulated some money and in 1972 bought

woodland, which at that time was cheap. He counted his purchase as an investment, but it was more than that. His interest
in forestry had become a passion, as it still is.

In college he majored in history, not forestry, which he
thinks was a good thing, for a person's education should be
broad rather than "vocational." As he went on with his work
in the woods, he realized that the conventional (and recommended) brand of forestry was wrong. It went against nature
and was not sustainable. I asked him how long it took him to
see this. He said, "Not long. It was obvious."

He had, he says, "no role model or mentor." Nor was he
acquainted with examples to show him what to try for. This
part of his education, the postgraduate part, was up to him.
He simply rejected the conventional practices and tolerances
that over time reduced the productivity of the forest, and
from there he was on his own. The change of mind from
forestry as an extractive industry to the study of sustainability
must always involve a radical shift in perspective. One ceases
to think of the source of sawlogs as trees, which can be cut
according to wishes or needs or standards that are merely
economic, and begins the understanding—far more complex
and difficult, but also far more interesting—that the source
is the forest ecosystem.

In 1985 Troy bought more woodland, and he has continued
to do so at the rate of "a property or two a year." He and his
wife, Lynn, got married in 1988. The wedding took place
on a beautiful day, out in the snowy woods, in January. Such

a wedding certainly suggests a strong liking for the woods, on the part of both bride and groom. And I would say that it suggests, more than most weddings, a strong mutual interest in getting married. Lynn and Troy have a daughter who, like Troy, is an only child.

Marriage and parenthood, for responsible people, lead to considerations of futurity and mortality, duties and limits. Troy and Lynn now had their daughter's future to think of, along with the future of their woodlands. This led them to the deliberations and arrangements of "estate planning." Like in fact a good many people, Troy thinks there ought to be a limit to a parent's bequest to a child. Too much makes things too easy. Eventually he asked his mother to change her will, removing him as her heir, and leaving her entire estate to his daughter. His mother's estate, he says, amounted to "something, not too much."

Providing for the future of the woodlands was a more difficult problem, for it involved more time, more unknowns, and evidently there were no precedents. Good management for the length of a human life is certainly a gift to the forest, but it is pathetically brief. A single tree may live several times as long as a human. A forest, kindly used, may outlive unimaginably any of its trees. Troy doesn't know whether he or his lawyer thought of it first, but the idea for the Firth Family Foundation emerged in 2004 from the need to provide the Firths' forest properties an inheritor that might keep them intact and

well managed beyond the limits of a human lifetime. This is
the same impulse that has led to the formation of land trusts
to hold development rights or "conservation easements" in
order to preserve farmland or open space beyond the lifetimes
of present owners. But Troy's vision for his foundation is more
complex, and it addresses more problems.

One of the most daunting problems in forestry, especially
in forested lands that are privately owned, is fragmentation.
Small holdings in farmland make sense, or can be made to
make sense. But small holdings in a forested landscape — and
the average privately owned forest acreage in Kentucky is just
under 20 acres; in Pennsylvania it is 16.7 — are too small both
economically and ecologically. A small woodlot on a farm can
contribute significantly to the economy and the life of the
farm, but a scattering of small forest properties, even if well
used, cannot sustain a forest ecosystem.

Another problem is short-term management of large tracts
of forest by financiers or investors who, for an acceptable
return in fifteen years, may highgrade their properties, or cut
everything, and then subdivide the land for "second homes."
The problem, predictably, is that "short term" land management leads almost inevitably to long-term exhaustion.

As the land resource declines, in forestry as in farming,
so necessarily does the local land economy and the local
human community. As the human community declines, there
are always fewer actual or potential good husbanders of the

land. As this cycle turns, whatever the nation and the national economy may be doing, the country and its native health and wealth spiral downward.

Troy understood that the good health and productivity of his own woodlands depends on good use sustained over a long time. But good health cannot be bounded and isolated like a property. The good health of part of a forest depends on the good health of the whole forest. It would not be enough for the foundation to serve merely as heir and steward of the Firths' personal holdings; the foundation could serve as an heir also to other forest owners, who might bequeath or donate their properties to it. Beyond that, the need is to exemplify and promote sustainable forestry for the sake of the forest ecosystem as a whole. The goal of the Firth Family Foundation was "to promote and practice long-term sustainable forestry while conserving working timberlands throughout Pennsylvania, New York and the surrounding states."

By 2010 the Firth Family Foundation had transformed itself into the Foundation for Sustainable Forests: A Land Trust. The name had become more general, but the regional boundary had been retained. Troy hopes that eventually there might be "numerous regional associations that could work cooperatively." The goal "is an abundance of intact forest ecosystems that provide for the widest range of native biodiversity possible, sustainable forest products, the economic viability of rural communities, and recreational opportunities."

What Troy had forming in his mind—what apparently is still forming in his mind—is the idea of a sustainable forest economy. Like any sustainable land economy, it would have to form locally, taking shape in response to local conditions, limits, and opportunities. The influence of its example and working principles would then extend to anybody who might be interested. Troy's ultimate wish is "to do whatever can be done to protect land." An example of sustainable forestry adapted to one place cannot be applied like a stamp to a different place. What *can* be applied are right principles and standards, and some understanding of what is involved in the effort of adaptation.

But a forest economy, however well adapted, however concordant with its ecosystem, cannot stand or continue alone. For a local economy to become truly sustainable, it must function as a belonging, a support and an artifact, of a local culture. The great need we are talking about is to hold the local forest ecosystem together, but that leads to a second need, just as great, which is to hold the local forest economy and therefore the local human community together. The two needs could be answered only by a thriving, confident, stable local culture in which the young would learn from their elders. Change and innovation would naturally occur, but would not be imposed from the outside or for the benefit primarily of outsiders. Nor would the changes and innovations arrive at the breakneck speed of industrial innovation. The community would understand that it exists, in part, to cherish the forest and to preserve its knowledge of the forest.

There is a good deal of supposing in that paragraph. In America, or in the history of Old World races in America, we have no example of an economic enterprise ecologically and socially sustainable. To imagine such a thing, we have to consult scattered pieces. Any conversation at home between grandparents and grandchildren is potentially the beginning of a local culture, even of a sustaining local culture, however it might be cut short and wasted.

Troy's practice of forestry, even when he was working mainly alone, was already one of the scattered pieces of a sustainable economy, and Troy knew that. But as he also knew, it was not nearly enough. He needed to be talking about his work with somebody, a younger somebody, at work with him. And so in 2005 he looked about in the Spartansburg area and hired Guy Dunkle, a bright young man just out of college, who, like Troy, was locally born and raised. I had gathered from my conversations with Troy that he had hired Guy as an apprentice or understudy, supplying the younger half of the necessary conversation. But when I asked the name of Guy's "position," hoping for better understanding, Troy said, not to my surprise, "We're not much on titles." He spoke of Guy simply as "a forester for Firth Maple Products." In the most practical terms, Guy is a younger forester coming behind an older forester and learning from him. "Everything depends on that," Troy said.

It is more than passingly significant, I think, that this complex enterprise of forestry, sawmilling, "maple products," and an emergent foundation is "not much on titles," and that its executive staff consists of two "foresters" involved in the fate of the same woodlands. It is significant also that Guy's college degree is in environmental science, not forestry, and that his job interview was conducted in the course of a week's work in the woods with Troy, tapping maple trees.

Guy Dunkle enjoys describing his job as whatever Troy doesn't much want to do. And so it was Guy who drove to Erie to meet my plane on May 16, 2012, when I came to walk and talk in the woods with the two of them and to take part in a couple of public events promoting the foundation. I had met Guy in October 2005 at one of Jason Rutledge's logging sites in Virginia, but our drive from the Erie airport to supper with Troy and Lynn Firth at their house was our first opportunity actually to become acquainted.

Guy is a tall, lean, pleasant man, impressive in several ways, not least for his apparent innocence of the too-common wish to "make an impression." He is not as quiet as Troy, but he is quiet enough. He seems, right away, to be a man of settled character, and you suppose he has answered several of the important questions about his life and his vocation. He and his wife, Wilma, have two young sons. They are living on their own farm, which is partly wooded, partly planted in Christmas trees, and partly in pasture. We spent a good many miles of our drive in a conversation about raising sheep. A young man with a farm, and fully interested in it, may be assumed to have some permanent intentions.

When we arrived at the house on Firth Road, Troy had come in from his day's work. Lynn gave us a good supper, most welcome to me, for my noon fare at the Cincinnati airport had been both meager and bad. I had asked Troy to show me as much of his practice of forestry as I would be able to see in the time available, and he had laid out a crowded itinerary. Soon after we had eaten, he and Guy and I used up the rest of the day on the first three stops of my tour of places important to see.

First we made a fairly quick drive-through at Troy's sawmill, most memorable to me for the ricks of beautiful large black cherry logs. To be profitable, a mill of this relatively small scale must have a specialty, or "niche," which here is the lucrative trade in veneer-quality cherry. That happens to be a proper niche for this area, which is uniquely productive of the finest cherry wood. To maintain the necessary stock of good logs, since he can't supply all he needs from his own relatively limited acreage, Troy regularly logs timber sales in the Allegheny National Forest or the Susquehannock State Forest.

We next went to the headquarters of Firth Maple Products, where the sap of thousands of trees is collected, reduced by boiling to the proper consistency of maple syrup, and bottled. My own country has a lot of sugar maples, but we have no tradition of syrup-making. We do, or did, have something of a tradition of sorghum molasses-making, and so I understand in principle the boiling down of a thin, mildly sweet liquid to a viscous liquid that is intensely sweet. But the equipment of Troy's maple syrup factory far exceeded in both scale and complexity any that I had seen before.

Troy's woodlands are full of pipelines. The black plastic pipe, most of it an inch and a quarter in diameter, is tightly stretched, reinforced by high-tensile, galvanized steel wire, and secured at about knee-height by other wires guyed to trees on either side. Small transparent tubes run the sap from the trees to the black pipes. I was impressed by the sturdiness of the pipelines, which are installed to last for several years, and also by the care with which they had been attached to the trees. Every wire that went around a tree was buffered by blocks of scrapwood to prevent injury to the bark. The pipelines carry the sap to tanks at well-sited collection points, from which it is trucked to the boilers. Troy is alert for any way to reduce costs. The maple syrup operation requires large tanks of various sizes and kinds, and many of these have been bought cheap—used or damaged but still good. The trucks are mostly stainless steel milk tankers, also used but good. If you have limited or no control of the markets you buy and sell on, thrift becomes an essential virtue.

Our third stop on the evening of my arrival was at a woodland that Troy had logged, he thought, ten times in the last forty-five years. And here we came to our principal subject and the purpose of my trip. Clearly, no patch of forest could have been so steadily productive for so many years if it had not been knowingly and carefully logged. And in fact this was an excellent demonstration of the results, over time, of worst-first single tree selection. The last cutting had been recent, the tops of the stumps were still bright and unweathered, and yet you could see immediately that the forest in that place was ecologically whole. There were no too-large openings in the canopy. The remaining trees were of a diversity of sizes, from large to small. None of the remaining trees had been damaged by the felling or skidding. Because the skidding had been done with horses, the ground had been only slightly scarred. The skid trails would mostly disappear by the next year.

My visit with Troy and Guy, and then with Jason Rutledge and his son Jagger, who arrived on Thursday afternoon, was from Wednesday evening until mid-morning on Sunday. Subtracting the several hours when we merely sat and talked, we probably spent two longish days walking, looking, and talking in the woods.

In the bright early sunlight of Thursday morning we walked into an open woodland of tall trees, and under them a uniform stand, virtually a garden, of graceful hay-scented ferns. This was a pleasant, "scenic" place where one might like to have a picnic, the sort of "natural" place that many a nature or wilderness enthusiast would like to "preserve." But there was a problem. There was no understory to speak of: no seedling trees, saplings, shrubs, or the smaller plants that in a thriving forest would occupy the spaces between the ground and the lower branches of the tallest trees. The succession of the trees had been broken. If one should be felled or blown down, there would be none to replace it. The culprit was the beautiful hay-scented fern, whose rhizomes and roots grow so thickly in the top layer of the soil that they cannot be penetrated by the roots of seedlings, and whose fronds steal the light from other plants.

This domineering population of ferns is caused by an overpopulation of white-tailed deer who eat and destroy the plants that compete with the ferns. Once the fern carpet is established, it remains dominant. Reducing the deer population then has no effect, and another remedy must be found. Among the ferns a few blackberry briars were scattered about, and these may offer some hope. It may be that where the blackberry roots have pierced the fern mat, the roots of other species may follow and take hold. Or it may be that the blackberries, because of their earlier leafing in the spring, will shade out the ferns. The interaction of the two species is as yet unclear. Alternatively, the ferns may have to be set back by the use of an herbicide. The immediate problem here for the long-term commercial forester—this is the point—is an ecological problem: how to restore to this impoverished woodland the highly diverse "vertical structure" indicative of ecological health.

The predominant and most valuable trees of this region are

black cherry and sugar maple. In addition, there are northern red oaks, some white oaks, white pines, and red or soft maples. Because of their yield of sap, the sugar maples have a special status in the Firth woodlands. They are dual-purpose trees. Tapping them for syrup degrades them somewhat as timber, but at appropriate times they too are logged.

But when you are with him in the woods, you can feel Troy's partiality for the tall, veneer-grade cherry trees with their dark, thick, flawless trunks. Looking with him at these trees, you see one of the primary ways in which good forest management increases yield. We were discussing a tall, thick-boled cherry tree with a fork at about half its height: two long, large prongs with many smaller branches. This woodland, Troy says, was highgraded perhaps ninety years ago. "High-grading," he says, "takes the top off the woods." This reduces the competition for space and light, with the result that the trees branch or fork lower than they normally or naturally would have done. This particular cherry is a valuable tree that will yield a log of high quality, but the main log will be half to two-thirds as long as it would have been in a properly managed forest. The tree, moreover, is vulnerable in a way that a single-stemmed tree is not. Cherry is a brittle wood. As the two great prongs of the fork become more top-heavy, and their leverage increases, it becomes more likely that they will cause the tree to break or split. A tree like this one must be closely watched. At some point, a skilled climber will top the tree so that it can be safely felled.

We visited, by contrast, a single-stemmed cherry tree in a woodland that had not been high-graded. This tree was perhaps ninety years old, about twenty inches in diameter at breast height, still flourishing, still making wood, and not nearly so old as, with right management, it may become. It was maybe a hundred and twenty feet tall, eighty feet to the first branch. Some day it will yield five sixteen-foot logs, the first two of veneer quality. It was by any measure a beautiful tree. We spent a good while looking up at it and complimenting it.

The great event of Friday morning was our encounter in the woods with two young Amish teamsters driving their two-horse teams from the high seats of the elegantly engineered carts known as "logging arches," which are used for skidding logs out of the forest. The carts are so constructed that, when the horses tighten against a log, the log's own weight causes its fore-end to lift off the ground, thus reducing friction, lightening the draft, and minimizing damage to the woods floor.

More remarkable were the two teams of horses that provide the traction power. These horses do the hardest sort of work daylong every weekday, drawing heavy loads over rough ground, and yet they had the appearance of show horses. They were sound, bright-eyed, in excellent flesh, their coats unflawed and shining. Their condition spoke well of everything involved, but principally of the intelligence, care, and skill of the two teamsters. These were friendly, articulate men in their late twenties or early thirties. In conversing with us, and particularly with Jason, who is himself an excellent horseman and teamster, they showed themselves to be constantly attentive to every point of contact between horse and harness. This comes from a fine kind of sympathy: A good horseman wants the horses to work as comfortably in their harness as he himself works in his clothes. Sometimes in horse logging one sawyer, felling the marked trees, will keep two or three teamsters busy skidding the logs out. Here, the teamsters themselves do the felling, and this gives an obvious advantage to the horses, who rest while the men work.

The use of horses in the woods is fundamental to Troy's way of logging. It may finally prove to be necessary to anybody's version of sustainable forestry. Horses are kinder to the forest than mechanical skidders. Their skid trails are narrower and require no digging or grading of the forest floor. Using less force, they are less violent. A horse's hooves may slip now and then, scarring the surface of the ground, but the wheels of a heavy skidder compact the soil and, in the roughest places, tend to dig. Horses, moreover, can work on wetter ground than skidders.

Horses and horse equipment also cost much less and work much cheaper than skidders, and this can yield a large advantage to the forest. A new skidder will cost in the neighborhood of $150,000, a used one something like $50,000. A teamster's outfit—horses, logging arch, chains, saw, etc.—might cost as little as $5,000. (The greatest "cost" of using horses is the knowledge of how to care for, breed, raise, train, and work them, which is now in short supply. But knowledge, once you know it, is free.) This is a significant and influential difference. The more expensive the logging equipment, the higher the operating costs, the greater must be the pressure to increase the daily volume of board feet, increasing in turn recklessness in the use of the forest and the likelihood of damage. The urge toward the highest possible volume works against selectivity, judgment, and forbearance. In forestry as in farming, low production costs can increase the quality of work and so of care for the land. The logger who is free of financial anxiety can stop and think.

Moreover, the use of horses in logging increases human employment. One person operating a skidder may replace three teamsters. We are taught to see that as an advantage, and it is, but only to the company that makes skidders, and to the suppliers of fuel. The advantages of horse logging, much to the contrary, accrue to the forest and the human community. The Amish horsemen we talked with earn a good living, working as "independent contractors." In a time officially obsessed with "job creation," perhaps we don't need to argue about the worth of three people in effect self-employed as opposed to one employee driving somebody else's machine. Horse logging, in addition, is principally maintained by the local economy, which in turn it helps to maintain, whereas the purchase of large machines and the fuel to run them siphons money out of the local economy to enrich the shareholders of remote corporations.

In keeping with his commitment to sustainability, Troy does what he can to favor continuity of employment. At present he has six teams at work in the woods. One of the teamsters, who happens to be one of Jason Rutledge's alumni, has worked for Troy for fifteen years, another for eight, two others for six. He tries to keep them busy all the year round. Except for times in the spring when the ground is too wet—and, when using horses, these times are not long—the logging is continuous. When it is too wet, Troy finds other work for the teamsters.

The connections and interactions among all the creatures in a thriving forest ecosystem are complex beyond the human ability to think. This is the starting point, the primary axiom. And so humility is the primary virtue of good forestry. One must get the scale right, so as not to put too much at risk. One must not use too much power, or be in too much of a hurry. Troy accordingly does not talk like an expert. Because the forest is complex, it requires a due complexity of knowledge and of thought. Ultimately it requires work that honors, not only the known complexity, but also the unknown, the mystery of the nature of any place. By now Troy has a lot of experience. He has thought and worked with care. But how does he know when he has worked well?

His summary statement to me was that he finds out from the songbirds. If one of his woodlands as a result of his care and management is ecologically healthy, if there is enough diversity of the species and ages of the plants from the lowliest flowers and shrubs to the tallest trees, if the "vertical structure" is right, then you will hear a lot of birds singing. This is not a Disney sentimentalism. The birds are not singing to compliment Troy. They are singing because they have found a diversity of places in which to nest and feed, as the nature of the forest requires. Their songs indicate that all, or at least enough, of the pieces are in place. They are singing specifically to Troy only in the sense that he knows at least this much of what they mean.

Another virtue essential to good forestry is generosity. You don't have to see much bad logging before you become unable to imagine that a selfish or greedy person could be a good forester. A good forester thinks first of the forest. I remember Troy saying at a forestry meeting several years ago, "A bad logger goes to the woods thinking of what he can take out. A good logger goes to the woods thinking of what he should leave." It is this generosity toward the forest that enables the necessary thought. Generosity involves the forester in the history of the forest, its past and its future.

Troy's knowledge of his woodlands is historical, extensive, highly particular, and intimate. If you follow him through the woods for several hours, you realize that you are passing through a succession of distinct places, each different from any other, in its community of plants, slope, exposure, soil quality, history, problems, and so on. About each place Troy is likely to know a more or less adequate history: from visible evidence, from local or personal memory, from dated aerial photographs. He will know that a given place, until a certain year, was cleared and farmed. Or he will know that another woodland was high-graded eighty years ago, or that another was carelessly logged fifty years ago. He is aware, of course, of general principles, ideas, and theories of forestry, some better than others, but he says, with emphasis, "Forestry is mainly observational, rather than theoretical." By "observation" Troy means walking and looking, paying attention, season after season, for many years. Eventually, a profound familiarity will grow between an observant forester and the places of the forest. Such knowledge is what we mean, maybe, by "sympathy" or "sixth sense" or "intuition." It is the knowledge that tells one, in a given situation, where to look or what to expect or how much is enough. It tells what to take and what to leave.

Though this certainly is knowledge, and though it certainly comes by a kind of education, it cannot be conveyed in courses or curricula or majors. This education is "observational" and it takes many years. To know competently a tract of forest, Troy says, "is going to take decades. That's all there is to it."

You can't learn one woodland by studying another, and you can load only a limited amount of competent or workable knowledge into one mind in one lifetime. This is why it is important for good foresters both to stay put and to have local successors. The United States Forest Service makes a practice of moving people around. We recognize this as an industrial

ideal: The supposedly easy mobility of human populations
is an exploitable asset. Troy's idea, on the contrary, is to stay
in place himself, and to hire local people for life. There is a
sound economic reason for this, in addition to its obvious
ecological value: Local knowledge of the local forest, like the
forest itself, is an asset.

A local or personal economy, no matter how intelligently and
kindly managed, cannot be made entirely immune to changes
in the larger economy, no matter how false or fantastical the
larger economy may be. And so in the "recession" that began
in 2008, Troy says, "I lost a bundle." His inventory of standing timber "fell off a cliff." Now things are improving, and
he recently hired two more skidding teams. In general the
Firth economy, within a larger economy never favorable to
the economies of land use, has done remarkably well. Probably the most interesting sentence in the circular issued by the
Firth Family Foundation is this: "A 2006 study by LandVest
showed that the Firths averaged 11 percent annual return on
their timberlands for the previous 20 years."

Troy Firth's years of work in the forest have carried him
far beyond the usual definitions of land ownership, of land
use, and even of forestry. Rather than requiring the forest to
submit to his economic demand, he has learned painstakingly
to fit his economy into the forest. He has taken his living from
the forest, not in defiance of the nature of the forest ecosystem, but to the best of his ability cooperating with it. Under

his management, the production of timber has not reduced the productivity of the forest. On the contrary, his management has increased productivity—it can, he says, almost double the production of poorly managed woodlands—at the same time that it increases the number of human workers. It would be hard to overestimate the importance of this, as an accomplishment and as an example: several human livelihoods taken from the forest, to the forest's benefit, which becomes in turn and complexly a further human benefit.

Troy is an exemplary user of the land. At a time when such exemplars are desperately needed, he is somebody to turn to for confirmation of certain good possibilities. But the value of this, as he well knows, is strictly limited. One or two good foresters here and there are not enough. Nor even would be some widespread brand of "sustainable forestry," given an official label in the fashion of "organic agriculture." To develop and promote a forest ethic would do some good, but it would not do much good in the absence of working and paying examples of good practice. Governments may provide some checks against bad forestry by laws, regulations, restraints, "incentives," etc., but governments do not have the means to bring about good forestry. In a note of June 25, 1942, Aldo Leopold recorded his sense of this governmental limit: "I am skeptical about government timber production as a sole remedy for the apathy of private timber owners."

A sustainable local forest economy would supply as many as possible of its own needs, and it would perform most of the value-adding to most of its products. A country-wide project of sustainable forestry would require for many years an increasing number of such economies, which would in turn depend on the coincidence of available decent livelihoods from the forest with the passion for forestry that came to Troy in his student days and has continued with him ever since. If you are not squeamish about the word, you might say the "love" of forestry. To say that the good care of the forest, as of all the world's places, depends upon love is, sure enough, to define a difficulty. But not an impossibility. The impossibility is that humans would ever take good care of anything that they don't love. And we can take courage from the knowledge that millions of Americans once loved their vegetable gardens, cared well for them, and kept them dependably productive—and that a good many still do.

The Foundation for Sustainable Forests, at present, is the work of a few people. It has so far acquired in its own name only 740 acres. It is assured eventually of having, by bequest from Troy and Lynn, more than 6,000 additional acres. What seems most hopeful about it is its solid basis in practicality. Unlike most foundations, this one will be a viable commercial enterprise. It can use donated money to purchase woodlands, but these properties will become self-sustaining.

Like The Land Institute, Tilth, the Quivira Coalition, the Southern Agriculture Working Group, the Land Stewardship Project, and other organizations concerned with sustainable agriculture, the Foundation for Sustainable Forests will occupy the intersection of ecology and economy, which ought to be occupied by everybody but at present has a surplus of elbow room. These organizations promoting sustainable land economies are identifiable by their endless agendas of work, by their virtual invisibility to the worlds of policy and the news, and by the swarms of questions that hover about them— questions asked and waiting for answers, questions as yet unasked.

For example: If sustainable forestry depends upon sustainable local forest economies, how will we develop the necessary small-scale value-adding industries? I don't know the answer, and I doubt that anybody does. But then I remember hearing that small Amish furniture factories did more than a hundred million dollars worth of business last year, and I draw another breath. The necessary pieces may already exist, though widely scattered and perhaps lost from one another. No one person will be capable of putting them all together. Troy Firth knows this, but he also knows a further truth: One person can begin. "And can begin better with the help of others."

4

Local Economies
to Save the Land
and the People

[2013]

As often before, my thoughts begin with the modern history of rural Kentucky, which in all of its regions has been deplorable. In my county, for example, as recently as the middle of the last century, every town was a thriving economic and social center. Now all of them are either dying or dead. If there is any concern about this in any of the state's institutions, I have yet to hear about it. The people in these towns and their tributary landscapes once were supported by their usefulness to one another. Now that mutual usefulness has been removed, and the people relate to one another increasingly as random particles.

To help in understanding this, I want to quote a few sentences of a letter written on June 22, 2013, by Anne Caudill. Anne is the widow of Harry Caudill. For many years she was involved in Harry's study of conditions in Eastern Kentucky and in his advocacy for that region. Since Harry's death, she has maintained on her own the long interest and devotion she once shared with Harry, and she is always worth listening to. She wrote:

> The Lexington Herald Leader last Sunday . . . published a major piece on the effects of the current downturn in the coal industry . . . Perhaps the most telling statement quoted came from Karin Slone of Knott County whose husband lost his job in the mines . . . finally found a job in Alabama and the family had to leave their home. Karin said, "There should have been greater efforts to diversify the economy earlier."
>
> [Fifty] years ago and more Harry tried . . . everything he could think of to encourage diversity. My heart goes out to those families who yet again are being battered by a major slump in available jobs. . . . Again they are not being exploited, but discarded.

This is a concise and useful description of what Anne rightly calls a tragedy, and "tragedy" rightly applies, not just to the present condition of Eastern Kentucky, but to the present condition of just about every part of rural Kentucky. The tragedy of Eastern Kentucky is the most dramatic and obvious because that region was so extensively and rapidly industrialized so early. The industrialization of other regions (mine, for example) began with the accelerated industrialization of agriculture after World War II, and it has accelerated increasingly ever since. The story of industrialization is the same story everywhere, and everywhere the result is ruin. Though it has developed at different rates of speed in different areas, that story is now pretty fully developed in all parts of our state.

To know clearly what industrialization is and means, we need to consider carefully some of the language of Anne Caudill's letter. We see first of all that she is speaking of a region whose economy is dependent upon "jobs." This word, as we now use it in political clichés such as "job creation," entirely dissociates the idea of work from any idea of calling or vocation or vocational choice. A "job" exists without reference to anybody in particular or any place in particular. If a person loses a "job" in Eastern Kentucky and finds a "job" in Alabama, then he has ceased to be "unemployed" and has become "employed," it does not matter who the person is or what or where the "job" is. "Employment" in a "job" completely satisfies the social aim of the industrial economy and its industrial government.

Perhaps there have always been "jobs" and "employees" to fill them. The point here is that the story of industrialization radically enlarges the number of both. It also enlarges the number of the unemployed and the unemployable. I can tell you confidently that the many owners of small farms, shops, and stores, and the self-employed craftspeople who were thriving in my county in 1945, did not think of their work as "a job." Most of those people, along with most skilled employees who worked in their home county or home town, have now been replaced by a few people working in large chain stores and by a few people using large machines and other human-replacing industrial technologies. Local economies, local communities, even local families, in which people lived and worked as members, have been broken. The people who once were members of mutually supportive memberships are now "human resources" in the "labor force," whose fate (to return to the language of Anne Caudill's letter) is either to be "exploited" by an employer or "discarded" by an employer when the economy falters or as soon as a machine or a chemical can perform their "job." The key word in Anne's letter is "discarded," which denotes exactly the meaning and the sorrow of our tragedy.

How can it be that the people of rural Kentucky can first become dependent upon officially favored industries, the "job-creating industries" that their politicians are always talking of "bringing in," and then by those industries be discarded? To answer that question, I need to refer again to Eastern Kentucky and something I learned there—or began consciously to learn there—nearly fifty years ago.

In the summer of 1965 I paid a visit of several days to my friend Gurney Norman, who was then a reporter for the *Hazard Herald*. At that time a formidable old man, Dan Gibson, armed with a .22 rifle, stopped a strip miner's bulldozer. The land Mr. Gibson was defending belonged to his stepson, who was serving with the Marines in Vietnam. Mr. Gibson's defiance and his arrest caused a considerable disturbance, and a crowd of troubled people gathered on a Friday night in the courthouse in Hindman. Gurney and I attended the meeting. That night Harry Caudill made a speech that recalled certain meetings in Philadelphia in the summer of 1776, for he spoke against the domestic successors of the British colonialists: "the mindless oafs who are destroying the world and the gleeful yahoos who abet them."

I am indebted to another speech of the same night. That speech was made by Leroy Martin, chairman of the Appalachian Group to Save the Land and the People. Mr. Martin bore witness to the significance of Dan Gibson's act, his loyalty, and his courage. He spoke impressively also of the forest that stood on the mountainside that Mr. Gibson had defended. He spoke the names of the trees. He reminded his hearers, many of whom were local people, that they knew the character and the value of such woodlands.

Three lines of thought have stayed with me pretty constantly from that time until now.

The first concerns the impossibility of measuring, understanding, or expressing either the ecological cost or the human heartbreak of the permanent destruction of any part of our only world.

The second consists of repeated returns to the impossibility, at least so far, of permanently stopping this permanent damage by confronting either actual machines or political machines. Dan Gibson's unlawful weapon was answered by the lawful weapons of thirteen state police, a sheriff, and two deputies. Our many attempts to confront the political machine that authorizes the industrial machinery have really not been answered at all. If money is speech, as our dominant politicians believe, then we may say that all our little speeches have been effectively answered by big money, which speaks powerfully though in whispers.

The third line of thought, the one I want to follow now, has to do with the hopefulness, and the correction, implied in the name of the Appalachian Group to Save the Land *and* the People. The name of that organization—and, if I have remembered it correctly, Leroy Martin's speech—assumed that we must not speak or think of the land alone or of the people alone, but always and only of both together. If we want to save the land, we must save the people who belong to the land. If we want to save the people, we must save the land the people belong to.

To understand the absolute rightness of that assumption, I believe, is to understand the work that we must do. The connection is necessary of course because it is inescapable. All of us who are living owe our lives directly to our connection to the land. I am not talking about the connection that is implied by such a term as "environmentalism." I am talking about the connection that we make economically, by work, by living, by making a living. This connection, as we see every day, is going to be either familiar, affectionate, and saving, or distant, uncaring, and destructive.

The loss of a saving connection between the land and the people begins and continues with the destruction of locally based household economies. This happens, whether in the United States after World War II or in present day China, by policies more or less forcibly moving people off the land. It happens also when the people remaining on the land are convinced by government or academic experts that they "can't afford" to produce anything for themselves, but must employ all their land and all their effort in making money with which to buy the things they need or can be persuaded to want. Leaders of industry, industrial politics, and industrial education decide, for example, that there are "too many farmers," and that the surplus would be "better off" working at urban "jobs." The movement of people off the land and into industry, away from local subsistence and into the economy of jobs and consumption, was one of our national projects after World War II, and it has succeeded.

This division between the land and the people has happened in all the regions of rural Kentucky, just as it has happened or is happening in rural places all over the world. The problem, invisible equally to liberals and conservatives, is that the forces that destroy the possibility of a saving connection between the land and the people destroy at the same time essential values and practices. The conversion of an enormous number of somewhat independent producers into entirely dependent consumers is a radical change that in many ways is immediately catastrophic. Without a saving connection to the land, people become useless to themselves and to one another except by the intervention of money. Everything they need must be bought. Things they cannot buy they do not have.

This great change is the subject of Harriette Arnow's novel *The Dollmaker*. In the early pages of this book we recognize its heroine, Gertie Nevels, as an entirely competent woman. Her competence does not come from any "success," political or social or economic. She is powerful because, within the circumstances of her agrarian life in the mountain community of Ballew, Kentucky, she is eminently practical. Among the varied resources of her native place, she is resourceful. She has, from her own strength and willingness and from her heritage of local knowledge, the means of doing whatever needs to be done. These are the means, for her, of being content in Ballew where she is at home. Her husband, Clovis, is not content or at home in Ballew. He is an off-and-on mechanic and coal hauler whose aspiration and frustration are embodied in a decrepit truck. This is during World War II. The world is changing, and people are being changed. Physically unfit for the draft, attracted to modern life and "big money," Clovis goes to Detroit and finds a job as a "machine repair man."

Gertie and their children follow him to the city where, to Gertie, the cars seem to be "driving themselves through a world not meant for people." They find that Clovis has rented a disheartening, small, thin-walled apartment, and is already in debt for a used car, a radio, and other things that he has bought on credit.

In these circumstances, Gertie's practical good sense is depreciated nearly to nothing, except for the meaning it gives to her grief. Back home, she had dreamed of buying, and had almost bought, a small farm that would have given greater efficacy to her abilities and greater scope to her will. As her drastically narrowed life in Detroit closes upon her, she thinks: "Free will, free will: only your own place on your own land brought free will." (And now we should notice that those who have lived in the saving way preferred by Gertie Nevels—and some have done so—are solvent still, and Detroit is bankrupt).

It is a small logical step from understanding that self-determination for an individual depends on "your own place on your own land" to understanding that self-determination for a community depends on the same thing: its home ground, and a reasonable measure of local initiative in the use of it. This gives us a standard for evaluating the influence of an "outside interest" upon a region or a community. It gives us a standard for evaluating the policy of "bringing in industry" and any industry that is brought in. Outside interests do not come in to a place to help the local people or to make common cause with the local community or to care responsibly for the local countryside. There is nothing at all to keep a brought-in industry in place when the place has become less inviting, less exploitable, or less profitable than another place.

We may not want to oppose any and all bringing in or coming in of industry, but localities and communities should insist upon dealing for themselves with any outside interest that proposes to come in. They should not permit themselves merely to be dealt *for* by state government or any other official body. This of course would require effective, unofficial local organizing, and I believe we are developing the ability to do that.

But the most effective means of local self-determination would be a well-developed local economy based upon the use and protection of local resources, including local human intelligence and skills. Local resources have little local value when they are industrially produced or extracted and shipped out. They become far more valuable when they are developed, produced, processed, and marketed by, and first of all to, the local people—when, that is, they support, and are supported by, a local economy. And here we realize that a local economy, supplying local needs so far as possible from local fields and woodlands, is necessarily diverse.

As things now stand, the land and people of rural Kentucky are not going to be saved by the state and the federal governments or any of their agencies and institutions. All of those great official forces are dedicated primarily to the perpetuation of the corporate economy, not to new life and livelihood in small Kentucky communities. We must not make of that a reason to give up our efforts for better politics, better policy, better representation, better official understanding of our problems and needs. But to quit *expecting* the help we need from government bureaus, university administrations, and the like will give us an increase of clarity and freedom. It will give us back the use of our own minds.

For the fact is that if the land and the people are ever to be saved, they will be saved by local people enacting together a proper respect for themselves and their places. They can do this only in ways that are neighborly, convivial, and generous, but also, and in the smallest details, practical and economic. How might they do this? I will offer a few suggestions:

1 – We must reject the idea—promoted by politicians, commentators, and various experts—that the ultimate reality is political, and therefore that the ultimate solutions are political. If our project is to save the land and the people, the real work will have to be done locally. Obviously we could use political help, if we had it. Mostly, we don't have it. There is, even so, a lot that can be done without waiting on the politicians. It seems likely that politics will improve after the people have improved, not before. The "leaders" will have to be led.

2 – We should accept help from the centers of power, wealth, and advice only *if*, by our standards, it is actually

helpful. The aim of the corporations and their political and academic disciples is large, standardized industrial solutions to be applied everywhere. Our aim, to borrow language from John Todd, must be "elegant solutions predicated on the uniqueness of [every] place."

3 – The ruling ideas of our present national or international economy are competition, consumption, globalism, corporate profitability, mechanical efficiency, technological change, upward mobility—and in all of them there is the implication of acceptable violence against the land and the people. We, on the contrary, must think again of reverence, humility, affection, familiarity, neighborliness, cooperation, thrift, appropriateness, local loyalty. These terms return us to the best of our heritage. They bring us home.

4 – Though many of our worst problems are big, they do not necessarily have big solutions. Many of the needed changes will have to be made in individual lives, in families and households, and in local communities. And so we must understand the importance of scale, and learn to determine the scale that is right for our places and needs. Brought-in industries are likely to overwhelm small communities and local ecosystems because both the brought-in and the bringers-in ignore the issue of scale.

5 – We must understand and reaffirm the importance of subsistence economies for families and communities.

6 – For the sake of cultural continuity and community survival, we must reconsider the purpose, the worth, and the cost

of education—especially of higher education, which too often leads away from home, and too often graduates its customers into unemployment or debt or both. When young people leave their college or university too much in debt to afford to come home, we need to think again. There can never be too much knowledge, but there certainly can be too much school.

7 – Every community needs to learn how much of the local land is locally owned, and how much is available for local needs and uses.

8 – Every community and region needs to know as exactly as possible the local need for local products.

9 – There must be a local conversation about how best to meet that need, once it is known.

10 – The high costs of industrial land-using technology encourage and often enforce land abuse. This technology is advertised as "labor-saving," but in fact it is people-replacing. The people, then, are gone or unemployed, the products of the land are taken by violence and exported, the land is wasted, and the streams are poisoned. For the sake of our home places and our own survival, we need many more skilled and careful people in the land-using economies. The problems of achieving this will be difficult, and probably they will have to be solved by unofficial people working at home. We can't expect a good land-based economy from people who wish above all to continue a land-destroying economy.

11 – The people who do the actual work and take the most immediate risks in the land economies have almost always

been the last to be considered and the poorest paid. And so we must do everything we can to develop associations of land owners and land users for the purpose of land use planning, but also of supply management and the maintenance of just prices. The nearest, most familiar model here in Kentucky is the federal tobacco program, which gave the same economic support to the small as to the large producers.

12 – If we are interested in saving the land and the people of rural Kentucky, we will have to confront the issue of prejudice. Too many rural Kentuckians are prejudiced against themselves. They have been told and have believed that they are provincial, backward, ignorant, ugly, and thus not worthy to "stand in the way of progress," even when "progress" will destroy their land and their homes. It is hard to doubt that good places have been destroyed (as in the coal fields) or appropriated by hostile taking (as in Land Between the Lakes) because, in official judgment, nobody lived there but "hicks" or "hillbillies." But prejudice against other disfavored groups still is alive and well in rural Kentucky. This is isolating, weakening, and distracting. It reduces the supply of love to our needs and our work.

To end, I want to say how grateful I am to have this audience for this speech. I remember when there was no organization called (or *like*) Kentuckians for the Commonwealth, and so I know its worth. I am proud to be one of you. In speaking to you, I've felt that I could reach, beyond several false assumptions, toward our actual neighborhoods and the actual ground under our feet. If we keep faithful to our land and our people, both together, never apart, then we will always find the right work to do, and our long, necessary, difficult, happy effort will continue.

Speech for Kentuckians for the Commonwealth
Carrollton, Kentucky, August 16, 2013

5

Less Energy,
More Life

[2013]

Like a lot of people I know, I am concerned about mountaintop removal and climate change. But when we delay our concern until dangers have become sensational we are late. Whether or not we are too late is a question that should not interest us. Even if we are too late, we still must accept responsibility and try to make things better.

In fact, mountaintop removal and climate change are not the sort of simple problems that can be solved by what we call problem-solving. They are summary evils gathered up from innumerable causes in the bad economy that we all depend upon and serve.

It is not as though we have not been warned. The advice against waste, extravagance, selfishness, arrogance, falsehood, and willful ignorance is old. But people of religion have generally entrusted questions about economy, about how we live, to economists and industrialists. Environmentalists seem to think that problems caused by technology can be solved, or "controlled," by more technology or "alternative" technology. People of both kinds seem to think that big problems have big solutions. Both are mistaken.

Fifty years ago Harry Caudill published *Night Comes to the Cumberlands*, causing a flurry of public attention and a spate of federal interest in solving "the problem of poverty" in the Appalachian coal fields. But that book describes the fundamental problem—which was, and is, the industrial plunder of the land and the people—and that problem, already long ignored by 1963, has continued to be ignored officially and conventionally for fifty more years. As Harry knew, and the politicians have not known, improving the health and economy of a region is not a one-issue project. It is not a one-solution problem.

The long-term or permanent damage inflicted upon all life, by the extraction, transportation, and use of fossil fuels is certainly one of the most urgent public issues of our time, and of course it must be addressed politically. But responsibility for the better economy, the better life, belongs to us individually and to our communities. The necessary changes cannot be made on the terms prescribed to us by the industrial economy and its so-called free market. They can be made only on the terms imposed upon us by the nature and the limits of local ecosystems.

If we are serious about these big problems, we have got to see that the solutions begin and end with ourselves. Thus we put an end to our habit of oversimplification. If we want to stop the impoverishment of land and people, we ourselves must be prepared to become poorer.

If we are to continue to respect ourselves as human beings, we have got to do all we can to slow and then stop the fossil fuel economy. But we must do this fully realizing that our success, if it happens, will change our world and our lives more radically than we can now imagine. Without that realization we cannot hope to succeed. To succeed we will have to give up the mechanical ways of thought that have dominated the world increasingly for the last two hundred years, and we must begin now to make that change in ourselves. For the necessary political changes will be made only in response to changed people.

We must understand that fossil fuel energy must be replaced, not just by "clean" energy, but also by *less* energy. The unlimited use of *any* energy would be as destructive as unlimited economic growth or any other unlimited force. If we had a limitless supply of free, nonpolluting energy, we would use the world up even faster than we are using it up now. If we are not in favor of limiting the use of energy, starting with our own use of it, we are not serious. If we are not in favor of rationing energy, starting with the fossil fuels, we are not serious. If we have the money and we are not willing to pay two dollars to keep the polluting industries from getting one, we are not serious. If, on the contrary, we become determined to keep the industries of poison, explosion, and fire from determining our lives and the world's fate, then we will steadfastly reduce our dependence on them and our payments of money to them. We will cease to invest our health, our lives, and our money in them. Then finally we will be serious enough, our effort complex and practical enough. By so improving our lives, we will improve the possibility of life.

Speech for a convention of Unitarians
Louisville, Kentucky, June 20, 2013

6

Caught in the Middle

[2013]

In the present political atmosphere it is assumed that everybody must be on one of only two sides, liberal or conservative. It doesn't matter that neither of these labels signifies much in the way of intellectual responsibility or that both are paralyzed in the face of the overpowering issue of our time: the destruction of land and people, of life itself, by means either economic or military. What does matter is that a person should choose one side or the other, accept the "thinking" and the "positions" of that side and its institutions and be so identified forevermore. How you vote is who you are.

We appear thus to have evolved into a sort of teenage

culture of wishful thinking, of contending "positions," over-simplified and absolute, requiring no knowledge and no thought, no loss, no tragedy, no strenuous effort, no bewilderment, no hard choices.

Depending on the issues, I am often in disagreement with both of the current political sides. I am especially in disagreement with them when they invoke the power and authority of government to enforce the moral responsibilities of persons. The appeal to government is made, whether or not it is defensible, when families and communities fail to meet their prescribed moral responsibilities. Between the two moralities now contending for political dominance, the middle ground is so shaken as to be almost no ground at all. The middle ground is the ground once occupied by communities and families whose coherence and authority have now been destroyed, with the connivance of both sides, by the economic determinism of the corporate industrialists. The fault of both sides is that, after accepting and abetting the dissolution of the necessary structures of family and community as an acceptable "price of progress," they turn to government to fill the vacancy, or they allow government to be sucked into the vacuum. This, I think, explains both Prohibition and the war on drugs, to name two failed government remedies. Another may be government-prescribed compulsory education.

To believe, as I do, that families and communities are necessary despite their present decrepitude is to be in the middle and to be most uncomfortable there. My stand nevertheless is practical. I do not think a government should be asked or expected to do what a government cannot do. A government cannot effectively exercise familial authority, nor can it effectively enforce communal or personal standards of moral conduct.

The collapse of families and communities—so far, more or less disguisable as "mobility" or "growth" or "progress" or "liberation"—comes from or with the collapse of personal character and is a social catastrophe. It leaves individuals subject to no requirements or restraints except those imposed by government. The liberal individual desires freedom from restraints upon personal choices and acts, which often has extended to freedom from familial and communal responsibilities. The conservative individual desires freedom from restraints upon economic choices and acts, which often extends to freedom from social, ecological and even economic responsibilities. Preoccupied with these degraded freedoms, both sides have refused to look straight at the dangers and the failures of government-by-corporations.

The Christian or social conservatives who wish for government protection of their version of family values have been seduced by the conservatives of corporate finance who wish for government protection of their semireligion of personal wealth earned in contempt for families. The liberals, calling for too few restraints upon incorporated wealth, wish for government enlargement of their semireligion of personal rights and liberties. One side espouses family values pertaining to temporary homes that are empty all day, every day. The other promotes liberation that vouchsafes little actual freedom and no particular responsibility. And so we are talking about a populace in which nearly everybody is needy, greedy, envious, angry, and alone. We are talking therefore about a politics of mutual estrangement, in which the two sides go at each other with the fervor of extreme righteousness in defense of rickety absolutes that are indefensible and therefore cannot be compromised.

Nowhere has this callow politics asserted itself more thoughtlessly and noisily than on the so-called rights of abortion and homosexual marriage. The real issue here is the politicization of personal or private life, and inevitably, given the absence of authentic political discourse or dialogue, the reduction of the issues to two absolute positions. In addition to distracting from interests authentically public and political, the politicization of personal life, involving as it must the publicization of privacy, is inhumane and inherently tyrannical.

After Boris Pasternak's *Doctor Zhivago* was published in the West and Pasternak received the Nobel Prize in 1958, thus earning the Soviet government's reprisal, Thomas Merton wrote:

> Communism is not at home with nonpolitical categories, and it cannot deal with a phenomenon which is not in some way political. It is characteristic of the singular logic of Stalinist-Marxism

that when it incorrectly diagnoses some phenomenon as "political," it corrects the error by forcing the thing to *become* political.
(*Disputed Questions*, p. 42)

Now, after many decades of anticommunism, Merton's sentences have come remarkably to be descriptive of our own politics. Maybe people who focus their minds for a long time upon enmity finally begin to resemble their enemies. This has happened before. It is deeply embedded in the logic of warfare.

Whatever the cause, we seem to have become as adept as the old Soviet Union at politicizing the nonpolitical. Most notably, by the connivances of both political sides, we have invented a sexual politics, which, by the standards of our own political tradition, is a contradiction in terms. Or it is if there is to be a continuing political distinction between public life and private life. This distinction, after all, is the basis of the freedoms protected by the First Amendment, which holds essentially that people's thoughts and beliefs are of no legitimate interest to the government. The government is not in charge of our personal lives, our private affections, our prayers, or our political opinions. It is not in charge of our souls. Those who formed our government also limited it, forbidding it any freehold in our homes or in our minds.

I am as ready as any so-called conservative to worry about big government, though I would remember that government has gotten big in the much-needed effort to regulate big corporations and to help their victims. To my fear of big government I add my at least equal fear of unlimited government, which is to say total government. It is not entirely surprising that after our long, costly resistance to communist dictatorship, we should now see the rise of passions and excuses tending toward capitalist dictatorship. The most insidious of these passions tends toward state religion and government regulation of private behavior.

Sexual politics has to do with public disagreements about rights that, however valid, are newly proclaimed, obscure in origin, extremely controversial, and productive of conflicts that probably are not politically resolvable—the prime example being the apparently unendable conflict over abortion.

Not so long ago abortion was illegal in the United States. It was illegal, one must suppose, because of an innate aversion to a woman's destruction of her own child. And then the Supreme Court ruled in *Roe v. Wade* (1973) that abortion, within certain limits, was legal. The ruling is based on the right to privacy under the 14th Amendment and, more remarkably and controversially, on the proposition that a human fetus is not legally a person and therefore is not eligible for the protections guaranteed by that amendment. This distinction between a fetus and a person is, to common sense, arbitrary and therefore inevitably a source of trouble. *Fetus*, to begin with, is a technical term which once was rarely used by pregnant women, who had conventionally and naturally referred to the creature forming in their wombs as a *baby*, which is to say a human being, a person. The abortion debate involves endless, unendable disagreement about such issues as when a fetus becomes a human or a person, when life begins, when or whether abortion should be legal, whether we should call it "killing" or "termination." Some enlightened people hold in derision the idea that life begins at conception. But if life does not begin at conception, then we are at the beginning of a kind of sophistry: an argument about when life may be *said* to begin.

The right to have an abortion has been popularly justified as a woman's right to control her own body. Such a right seems to be implied by a number of other rights, but only recently has it been stated in this way. So stated, it is somewhat confusing, for many of our laws, legal and moral, *require* one to control one's body—to restrain it, for instance, from killing the body of another person, except of course when ordered to do so by the government. To say when and why a requirement may become a right, and when and why the requirement or the right should be suspended or opposed, needs a lot of spelling out—if such a spelling out is possible.

The facts remain, on one side, that abortions are still proscribed by some religious traditions and the old aversion is still felt by many people, and, on the other side, that the legalization of abortion answers a need desperately felt for real and pressing reasons by many women, and legal abortion would at least put an end to illegal abortions badly performed in bad circumstances by incompetent and disreputable people.

Also involved are questions of ultimate seriousness and importance: questions of life and death that exceed the competence of human intelligence and are forever veiled in mystery. The trains of causation run quickly out of sight. I know a man who said, plausibly, "Life begins with erection." Elders used to refer young people to a time "when you were just a look in your mother's eyes." But when I asked the geneticist Wes Jackson, "Does life begin at conception?" he replied, "Life *continues* at conception." This, I felt, was at last a statement sufficiently serious.

In making any choice, we choose for the future, and so all our choices involve us in mystery and in a kind of tragedy. To choose to have a baby, to abort a fetus, to save a life, to destroy a life is to make a whole change on the basis of partial knowledge. One chooses in light of what one knows now about the past and thus changes the future inevitably and forever. What would have been, had the choice been different, will never be known.

To reduce this complexity and mystery to a public contest between two absolutes seems to wrong everything involved. Some equivocation seems natural and appropriate because one is attending to two possibilities, both unknown. Saints, heroes, great artists and scientists began as fetuses. So did tyrants, torturers, and mass murderers. Choices do not invariably cut cleanly between good and evil. Sometimes we poor humans must choose between two competing goods, sometimes between two evils. Responsibility or circumstances will require us to choose. But we cannot choose to be unbewildered or not to grieve.

The theologian William E. Hull, worrying over the destructive animosities that divide religious organizations, asked, "How can we avoid the wrangling that breeds hostility?" And he answered: "By seeking clarity rather than victory" (*Beyond the Barriers*, p. 169). This sounds exactly right to me, and I find little clarity in the public argument about abortion. I know that both sides are made up of individual humans whose thoughts and feelings may differ in significant ways from the public positions of their sides. But the problem with those positions as they are generalized and vented into the political atmosphere is that they substitute simplicity for clarity. By separating the statistical facts of abortion from the lived experience—from the mystery, bewilderment, and suffering that attend it—the simplicity becomes obscure and heartless. To the proabortion side, abortion is simply a right, the creature to be aborted is a fetus, the act itself is termination of a pregnancy by a forthright medical procedure. To the antiabortion side, abortion is simply a wrong to be refused or opposed in obedience to a moral or religious law that ought to be the law of the land. The two sides seem about equally to disregard both the truth of human suffering and the possibility of human compassion. Sexual politics is overflowing with principles and abstractions, but otherwise seems deserted. No actual woman wanting or needing or refusing an abortion is present.

The issue, I think, can be clarified only by imagining a woman to whom an abortion is one of two heartbreaking alternatives, one of which she alone must choose, and between which, however she chooses, she will remain emotionally divided perhaps for the rest of her life. This woman, troubling as she is to the political atmosphere of opposed absolutes, cannot be admitted by either side into the public argument. But her example is starkly clarifying. Her absence from the argument stupefies both sides.

I am unsure of the whereabouts or even the possibility of truth in the abortion strife, but I, with perhaps a good many others, am somewhere in the middle, where I see no chance of a public reconciliation. In fairness, we have to acknowledge that within the experience and history of abortion there must be many shades and mixtures of right and wrong. As in the human condition generally, we are not dealing with a choice between a shadowless light and utter darkness.

I have said several times that I am opposed to abortion except when it is necessary to save the mother's life. I stick to that, for I still feel strongly the old aversion. Unlike the proabortion side, I think that abortion is killing. What else could it be? And I think that the creature killed is a human being, for it can be a being of no other kind, and it is not a nonbeing. But I feel just as strongly an aversion to our life-destroying economy and way of life, and every day increases our need to cherish life in all its forms. I oppose the official killings that bear the names of justice and defense and also the killing that is a cost or by-product of certain industrial enterprises. I do, however, recognize the cruelty that is inherent and inescapable in the life of this world, in which no creature lives but at the expense of other creatures, as I recognize right and wrong ways of exacting and recompensing such costs.

But when I have spoken of my opposition to abortion, I hope I have never neglected to say that I can imagine circumstances in which I would willingly aid and comfort a girl or a woman getting an abortion. And here I arrive at what is for me the moral difficulty, even the moral obscurity, of this problem: Though I can say that, in some circumstances, I would willingly help somebody get an abortion, I cannot say that I would willingly aid and abet a murder.

Whatever one may think of a woman's right to control her own body, the inexpressibly intimate involvement of her own body in a woman's decision to have an abortion is a real and urgent consideration, and for a man it is a special one. That it does not involve, and could never have involved, my body does not invalidate my belief that abortion is wrong, but it does require me to be carefully aware of the bodily difference. Whereas a person's demonstrated willingness to kill another person already born requires us to look upon that killer as a public menace, a woman's decision to kill the baby in her womb does not require us to look upon her as a menace to anybody else. In fact we *don't* look upon her in that way.

So far as I can see, there are four possible legislative choices in relation to the abortion controversy:

1. Abortion could be forbidden absolutely, with no exceptions.
2. It could be forbidden, with specified exceptions.
3. It could be permitted, with specified exceptions.
4. We could permit it without exception, which to me means that we would have no law related specifically to abortion.

The first of these would outrage the proabortion side, it would settle the controversy merely by ignoring it, it is immitigably harsh, and it makes little sense. Absolute forbidding would choose the life of the unborn child over any and all other considerations, including that of the mother's life. The government thus would abandon any obligation to protect the mother's life in order to protect the life of the child. If, for want of an abortion, mother and child *both* should die, then the state would accomplish no good at all except for the pacification of fanatics.

Any law forbidding abortion would be ineffective, and it could easily do harm. To forbid an established practice for which the demand is widespread and the supply dispersed and readily available would be virtually to license an illicit and lucrative economy that would reward the greed and enterprise of the worst people. It would repeat the futility of the War on Drugs and Prohibition. Such a situation undermines government authority and brings law enforcement into disrespect.

The two middle solutions, as opposed to an outright ban, would require niggling official regulation of the conduct of individual persons, conduct at least semiprivate. This would require an increase in police power that would be expensive and also a danger to everybody's freedom. We could, for example, make a law forbidding abortion except to save the mother's life, but what would we mean by "the mother's life"? Would it be denoted only by her vital signs or, more reasonably, by her ability to live and thrive in the world—in which case the definition of her life would include her economic life, the life of her family (if she has one), even the life of her community (if she has one). For another example, we could make a law permitting abortion except during the third trimester. But this would require a lot of official watching. And who is to say exactly when the third trimester begins? Such legislating can only strand everybody, including the government, in permanently painful and dangerous confusion.

The problem in forbidding or permitting with exceptions is that the exceptions apparently cannot be decided upon by precise determinants, but rather by "approximate" or "appropriate" judgments by experts. The language of *Roe v. Wade*, as the ruling implicitly acknowledges, is vague and uneasy. What exactly is meant, with respect to abortion, by *life, conception, viability, privacy,* and *person? Roe v. Wade* does not, to my mind, settle the meaning of any of those words. The legal definition of a person evaporated when the Supreme Court defined a corporation as a person. If a corporation is a person, contrary to all previous usage and to common sense, then personhood can be conferred upon virtually anything merely by decree. Issues are thus quickly carried not just into vagueness but beyond the bounds of language.

I am going to take the risk, therefore, of saying that there should be *no* law either for or against abortion. Like certain other wrongs—various addictions, let us say—this one is more personal than public and would be best dealt with by the persons immediately involved: the pregnant girl or woman, her family or her friends, her doctor.

This is my attempt to make a statement on abortion that is reasonably complete—and that, in result, may be necessarily incomplete. I should add that I may find further reasons that will require me to revise. To have a mind, I think, depends upon one's willingness to change it.

Regarding homosexual marriage, the fault that I again must acknowledge is that what I have said before has been incomplete. As far as I remember, I have made only two public statements about this issue. My argument, much abbreviated both times, was that sexual practices of consenting adults ought not to be subjected to the government's approval or disapproval and that domestic partnerships, in which people who live together and devote their lives to one another, ought to receive the spousal rights, protections, and privileges that the government allows to heterosexual couples.

In those two statements I was considering homosexual marriage as an issue of law—with reference to the contention from both sides that marriage is a right to be granted or withheld by the government. This puts me again in the middle but this time with more certainty of my whereabouts and with good reasons to object.

First, this "right to marriage" is still birth-wet. It exists only to be selectively withheld. Apart from its momentary political expediency there is no reason for it. Whatever one may think of all that is presently implied and entailed by the legalization of marriage, surely nobody can claim that marriage is either the government's invention or that the government has an inherent right to determine who may marry. A government that can forbid two women or two men to marry might with better reason forbid two bigots to marry.

Second, this right depends upon a curious agreement between liberals and conservatives that human rights originate in government, to be dispensed to the people according to their pleading and at the government's pleasure, implying inescapably that any right, being so expediently the government's gift, can just as expediently be withheld or withdrawn. This flatly contradicts the founding principle of American democracy that human rights are precedent to the government's existence, that the government is established to protect them, and that the government must be restrained from violating them.

Third, it cannot be allowable, under the above principles, for the government, on the pleading of *some* of the people, to establish a right solely for the purpose of withholding it from some other people. If this were to happen, it would amount to a punishment imposed on a disfavored group for no crime except their existence. I don't need to point out that this has happened before.

That the liberals, who so often have been rightly anxious about the protection of rights and liberties, should define those rights and liberties as the gifts of a generous and parental government is absurd.

The conservative program on this issue, promoting as it does a constitutional apportionment of rights according to sexual category, in implicit violation of the Fifteenth and Nineteenth Amendments, is more darkly absurd. The theory that accreditation of the sexual practices of individuals is a function proper to a "small" and noninterfering government is comical.

That homosexuals have been denied the right to marry, supposing for the moment that such a right can exist, surely violates the Fourteenth Amendment, which forbids the state to "deprive any person of life, liberty, or property, without due process of law; [or] to deny to any person within its jurisdiction the equal protection of the laws." There is no need for homosexuals to be granted a right to marry that is at all different from the right of heterosexuals to do so. There is no good reason for the government to treat homosexuals as a special category of persons.

To support their strategy of outlawing homosexual marriage, Christians of a certain disposition have found several ways to categorize homosexuals as a different kind from themselves, who are in the category of heterosexuals and therefore normal and therefore good. They are mindful that the Bible looks upon homosexual acts as sinful or perverse. But it is not clear to me why perversion should have been specifically assigned to homosexuality. The Bible has a lot more to say against fornication and adultery than against homosexuality. If one accepts the 24th and 104th Psalms as scriptural norms, then surface mining and other forms of earth destruction clearly are perversions. If we take the Gospels seriously, how can we not see industrial warfare and its unavoidable massacre of innocents as a most shocking perversion? By the standard of all scripture, neglect of the poor, of widows and orphans, of the sick, the homeless, the insane, is an abominable perversion. Jesus taught that hating your neighbor is tantamount to hating God, and yet some Christians hate their neighbors as a matter of policy and are busy hunting biblical justifications for doing so. Are they not perverts in the fullest and fairest sense of that term? And yet none of these offenses, not all of them together, has made as much political-religious noise as homosexual marriage.

Another way to categorize and isolate homosexuals from the general citizenry and the prerogatives of citizenship is to define homosexuality as a disease having a cause that can be discovered and removed or cured by some sort of therapy. This seems most promising as long-term job security for scientists and doctors. Ken Kesey once saw an inscription in a men's room: "My mother made me a homosexual." Under it somebody else had written: "If I gave her the yarn would she make me one?" My own speculation is that we will never do much better than that. We will discover that, like all the rest of us, homosexuals are made what they are by their mothers, their fathers, their genes, their germs, their upbringing and their education, by their friends and neighbors, their dwelling places, their time and its culture, by their economic and social status, their personal history, and by history.

Yet another such argument is that homosexuality is unnatural. If the nature in question is merely biological—the realm of the ape and the naked ape—that may prove too roomy and accommodating to be of much help. By the standard of that nature, monogamy is unnatural, an artifact of *some* cultures. If it is argued that homosexual marriage cannot be reproductive, is therefore unnatural and should be forbidden, must we not then argue that any childless marriage is unnatural and should be annulled?

Specifically *human* nature, by contrast, has always had a

definition more complex and demanding than that of a naked ape. William Blake thought we are made human by being made in the image of God:

> For mercy, pity, peace, and love
> Is God our father dear;
> And mercy, pity, peace, and love
> Is man, his child and care."
>
> (*Songs of Innocence*, XX)

Are homosexuals capable of mercy, pity, peace, and love? Some certainly are, as some heterosexuals certainly are. To deny that distinction to homosexuals is to deny categorically that they are human, which is hardly a proper employment for mercy, pity, peace, and love. Oversimplified moral certainties—always requiring hostility, always potentially violent—isolate us from mercy, pity, peace, and love and leave us lonely and dangerous. The only perfect laws are absolute, but perfect laws are only approximately fitted to imperfect humans. That is why we have needed to think of mercy, and of the spirit, as opposed to the letter, of the law.

One may find the sexual practices of homosexuals to be unattractive or displeasing and therefore unnatural. But anything that can be done in that line by homosexuals can be done, and is done, by heterosexuals. Do we need a political remedy for this? Would conservative Christians like a small government bureau to inspect, approve, and certify their sexual behavior? Would they like a colorful tattoo, verifying government approval, on the rumps of lawfully copulating persons? We have the technology, after all, to monitor everybody's sexual behavior, but so eager an interest in other people's most private intimacy is both prurient and totalitarian.

The oddest of the strategies to condemn and isolate homosexuals is to propose that homosexual marriage is opposed to and a threat to heterosexual marriage—as if the marriage market is about to be cornered and monopolized by homosexuals. If this is not industrial-capitalist paranoia, it at least follows the pattern of industrial-capitalist competitiveness, according to which you *must* destroy the competition. If somebody else wants what you've got—from money to marriage—you must not hesitate to use the government (small, of course) to keep them from getting it.

But if heterosexual marriage is so satisfying to heterosexual couples, why can they not just reside in their satisfaction? So-called traditional marriage, now mostly divested of a traditional household and traditional bonds to a community, is for sure suffering a statistical failure, but this is not the result of a homosexual plot. Heterosexual marriage does not need defending. It only needs to be practiced, which is pretty hard to do just now. But the difficulty is rooted mainly in the values and priorities of our industrial-capitalist system, in which every one of us is complicit.

———

It certainly is possible for a government to withhold the legal perquisites of marriage from any group that it may be persuaded to designate in our present civil cold war. That is mainly to say that a government can forbid its officers to license weddings for people in the designated group.

But a wedding is not a marriage. A wedding is traditionally an exchange of vows of fidelity and love in all circumstances until death. In some circumstances, for some people, a wedding may be a sacrament. But however complicated and costly the preparations, the costumes, the photography, and the reception, a wedding is over and done with in a few minutes.

A marriage, by contrast, is the *making* of marriage, by daily effort to live out the vows until death. The vows may be taken seriously or not, broken or not, but there is no way of withholding them from homosexuals. You cannot copyright the vows, which a homosexual couple is perfectly free to make. The government cannot forbid them to do so, nor can any church.

Conjugal love, Kierkegaard wrote,

> is faithful, constant, humble, patient, long-suffering, indulgent, sincere, contented, vigilant, willing, joyful. All these virtues have the characteristic that they are inward qualifications of the individual. The individual is not fighting with external foes but fights with himself. . . . Conjugal love does not come with any outward

sign . . . with whizzing and bluster, but it is the imperishable
nature of a quiet spirit.

(*Either/Or*, in *A Kierkegaard Anthology*,
edited by Robert Bretall, pp. 89–90)

No church can *make* a homosexual marriage, because it cannot make any marriage, nor can it withhold any degree of
blessedness or sanctity from any pledged couple striving day
by day to be at one. If I were one of a homosexual couple, the
same as I am one of a heterosexual couple, I would place my
faith and hope in the mercy of Christ, not in the judgment
of Christians.

Condemnation by category is the lowest form of hatred, for
it is cold-hearted and abstract, lacking the heat and even the
courage of a personal hatred. Categorical hatred is the hatred
of the mob, which makes cowards brave. And there is nothing
more fearful than a religious mob overflowing with righteousness, as at the crucifixion, and before, and since. This sort of
violence can happen only after we have made a categorical
refusal of kindness to heretics, foreigners, enemies, or any
other group different from ourselves.

Kindness is not a word much at home in current political and
religious speech, but it is a rich word and a necessary one.
There is good reason to think that we cannot live without it.
Kind is obviously related to *kin*, but also to *race* and to *nature*.
In the Middle Ages *kind* and *nature* were synonyms. *Equal*, in

the famous phrase of the Declaration of Independence, could be well translated by these terms: All men are created kin, or of a kind, or of the same race or nature.

Jesus saves the life of the woman taken in adultery by removing her from the category in which her accusers (another mob) have placed her and placing her within kindness, his own kindness first and then that of her accusers: "He that is without sin among you, let him first cast a stone at her."

The accusers take this kindness as a defeat, as we all are too likely to do, and they depart without another word. The brief dialogue that follows is wonderfully animated by Jesus's sense of humor:

> "Woman, where are those thine accusers? hath no man condemned thee?"
>
> "No man, Lord."
>
> "Neither do I condemn thee: go, and sin no more."
>
> (John 8:7, 10–11)

Good advice—but can we suppose he could have given it without smiling, knowing as he did the vast repertory of sins and the endless human susceptibility?

Within the larger story of the Gospels this story is not exceptional. It does show us Jesus's way of dealing with one of the biblically denominated sins, but he simply reaches out to the woman in her great need as he did many times to many others. In the Gospels the sinfulness of all humans is assumed. It is neediness that is exceptional, and in Jesus's ministry need clearly takes a certain precedence over sin. His kindness is best exemplified by his feedings and healings with no imputation at all of deserving.

But the wealth of this idea of kindness is not exhausted by kindnesses to humans. It is far more encompassing. From some Christians as far back as the twelfth century, certainly from farther back in so-called primitive cultures, and from some ecologists of our own time, we have the idea of a great kindness including and binding together all beings: the living and the nonliving, the plants and animals, the water, the air, the stones. All, ultimately, are of a kind, belonging together, interdependently, in this world. From the point of view of Genesis 1 or of the 104th Psalm, we would say that all are of one kind, one kinship, one nature, because all are *creatures*.

Much happiness, much joy, can come to us from our membership in a kindness so comprehensive and original. It is a shame, as I know from long acquaintance with myself, to be divided from it by the autoerotic pleasure of despising other members.

7

On Receiving One of
the Dayton Literary
Peace Prizes

[2013]

WHEN WE WERE notified of this award my wife,
Tanya Berry, uttered a sound that closely resembled laughter.
She better than anybody knows how willingly I have risked
controversy, and how much I have enjoyed it, especially when
I was young. In my favor I can only say that I have never killed
or physically harmed any of my enemies, or wished to do so,

and that I don't carry a pistol. The only thing I would really enjoy shooting is a drone.

I am of course grateful for this award and all that it means. And I am of course necessarily humbled and somewhat troubled by it. There is something a little odd, after all, in giving an award associated with peace to any member of an industrial society, for the industrial economy, from agriculture to war, is by far the most violent the world has ever known, and we all are complicit in its violence. Our prevalent ways of using our land—land use plus industrial technology, minus care—produce commodities highly profitable to corporations at the unaccounted cost of massive waste and destruction. Our ways of war—politics minus neighborly love, plus industrial technology—are ever more profitable to corporations and ever more massively wasteful and destructive. Because these ways are so immensely profitable, their political and scientific defenders are accredited by wealth and power, hence by respectful listeners. Advocates for kinder ways are mostly unheard.

There is in fact no significant difference of means between weapons of massive destruction and the technologies of industrial production. The means invariably are combustion (internal and external) and poison (by intention, accident, or "act of God"). In order to mine a seam of coal in eastern Kentucky and West Virginia, we destroy a mountain, its topsoil, and its forest with no regard for the ecosystem, or for the people downhill, downstream, and later in time. The difference between blasting in the coal fields and erosion in the corn and soybean fields is only that erosion is slower. The end—the exhaustion of nature's life-supporting systems—is the same. But this should not surprise us if we have understood at all the history of industrial war. In his ironically titled book, *Freedom from Fear*, David M. Kennedy wrote that "by August 1945 the atomic bombs hardly represented a moral novelty. The moral rules that had once stayed men's hands from taking up weapons of mass destruction against non-combatants had long since been violently breached in World War II, first in the aerial attacks on European cities, then even more wantonly in the systematic firebombing of Japan." He might have added other instances of such destruction in that war by our enemies, our allies, and ourselves. Beyond the scope of Prof. Kennedy's book the instances of this disregard go on and on, always elaborately justified as national righteousness and the defense of freedom. In the accounting of our wars, we speak often of the "human cost" to our side, the lives of young people spent, as we say, in defense of "our way of life." We speak little of the "human costs" and "collateral damages" paid by our enemies. We speak almost never of the ecological costs of industrial war, which we must assume to be as great, as "unsustainable," as the ecological costs of industrial land use.

But surely, by now, the official rationalizations of our

violence have become too obviously hypocritical to be ignored. Violence against our world and our fellow beings finally cannot be dissociated from the violence of falsehood.

How can we continue to insist that our land-destroying, water-and-air-polluting agriculture is the *only* way to "feed the world," especially since we have now devoted so much of it to "biofuels" to feed our automobiles?

How can we assume that the world can be fed by an agriculture that continues to assign the greatest risks, the lowest income, and no regard at all to the primary producers?

Why should we think that high rates of production can be maintained when the land is increasingly degraded and ever fewer farmers' children want to farm?

Moreover: Why should we continue to believe to that *our* government is uniquely to be trusted with *our* weapons of mass destruction, whereas other nations are not to be trusted with theirs?

What does trustworthiness mean in relation to the possession of such weapons?

Why is the cost of our wars now paid almost exclusively by the young people in the armed services, who must pay with their bodies and their lives?

Why don't our patriotic citizens and their representatives insist upon the tax increases necessary to support our wars?

Why do they not curtail by rationing or other means our extravagant consumption of the fuels and materials necessary to our wars?

Why do not our patriotic trustees of the common good, upon consenting to a war, not resign from their offices and volunteer to put their own "boots on the ground"?

Such questions no doubt are merely naïve. Surely prevarication, bad faith, self-serving, ignorance, and nonsense must be normally and expectably among the costs of representative government. Surely despite such frailties, but assisted by the will of God and His prejudice in our favor, our rights will be preserved and our freedoms will endure.

We speak of freedom, of our God-given freedom, of defending, using, and enjoying freedom, as of something memorized in grade school and never thought about again. We might as well be talking in our sleep. We have been so thoughtless and careless of our freedom for so long that by now we cannot see that our assumed right to be limitlessly violent would finally bring us to a violence against freedom that may destroy it,

I am speaking of our present massive effort of so-called national security, comprised of an immense force of secret police, regulated by processes and persons equally secret, and possessing a gigantic technology of surveillance, also secret, which it has used to intrude into the private communications of every citizen of our own country and evidently of every citizen in the world who has the misfortune to possess a telephone or a computer, and all of this with no hint of probable cause, and without a sham or shadow of due process.

A people inured to violence even as entertainment may

have difficulty in seeing such an unassertive (so far) enterprise of "security" as violent. After all, we would not yet even have heard of it had not an alleged "criminal," by an exemplary act of citizenship, apprised us of its existence. But of course it is violent. Under our system of government, it is violent in its conception and purpose. It violates the Fourth Amendment's guarantee of "the right of the people to be secure in their persons, houses, papers, and effects, against unreasonable searches and seizures . . ." It violates our most intimate and natural sense of personal privacy that is the source and justification of the Fourth Amendment. It is a flagrant insult, legally, to our Constitution and, personally, to ourselves. It is a blatant assertion of absolute and unquestionable power, exactly the totality of government that we have claimed to be opposing in all the wars of my lifetime. And of course every imaginable violence is potential in it.

Almost as dismaying as this secretive and tyrannous "security" is the talk among people reputedly intelligent of "the need to balance freedom and security." "Balance" is an unfortunate word here, for it raises two extremely perilous questions: Who is to load the scales? and Who is to position the fulcrum? In our customary glibness about freedom, are we now supposing that it is a substantial commodity, some of which can be portioned off and exchanged for another commodity called "security"? But there can be no balance between freedom and secret police, universal suspicion, and tyranny. There is only a choice. If we have the courage, we will choose freedom, and we will use it to oppose our government's frivolous and dangerous secrecy, which it imposes upon us under the claim of "security" but really to hide its abuse of power and its shame. Peace comes from freedom, *real* freedom. It comes from responsibility, real *acceptance* of responsibility.

Freedom is not simple, for it always is involved with responsibility. The relation between freedom and responsibility is not a "balance" to be expediently adjusted by governments or citizens, who without both can have neither. I have quoted John Milton's definition of freedom before, and I am going to quote it again, for it is complex and precise enough to have the force of an essential justice: "To be free," Milton wrote, "is precisely the same thing as to be pious, wise, just, and temperate, careful of one's own, abstinate from what is another's and thence, in fine, magnanimous and brave."

Speech given at Dayton, Ohio, November 3, 2013

8

Our Deserted Country

[2014]

I.

IF WE ARE to understand the history of our landscapes, which mostly are economic—farms, ranches, working forests, mines—we will have to begin by understanding
the impetus and motive of the Industrial Revolution. Many
people, still, will regard this suggestion as odd or unthinkable,
though even some economists have begun to acknowledge
what has always been obvious: One result of replacing human
workers by industrial technologies is "joblessness."

But joblessness has been exactly the aim of industrialization from its beginning, as the so-called Luddites understood immediately. The purpose of industrial technology has always been to cheapen work by displacing human workers, thus increasing the flow of wealth from the less wealthy to the more wealthy. We have dealt with the violence always implicit in these substitutions by disregarding it, or disguising it by an official, quasi-religious litany of synonyms: *labor-saving, efficiency, progress, convenience, speed, comfort,* even *creative destruction.* Maybe we have to grant the possibility of some degree of altruism. Painless dentistry is often invoked as a justification of technological progress, and surely we must concede that painlessness is preferable to pain, just as comfort is preferable to discomfort. But what might be the costs of the "God-wrought" painlessness and comfort that have come with industrialization? "There is no such thing as a free lunch," the hard-headed realists love to advise us, implying that they have completely "done the numbers." But actually in all the industrial world the least popular mathematical operation is subtraction. We habitually imply that all the gains of technological progress are entirely net. *Our* painlessness and comfort are *everybody's* painlessness and comfort. Nobody pays, nobody loses.

But obsolescent human workers, characteristically, have been both replaced and displaced. The costs of progress have routinely been borne by discarded workers, and often the costs have been exorbitant. Of the outmoded coal miners of eastern Kentucky, Harry Caudill wrote:

Many voices have decried [mechanization], contending . . . that when machines relegate men to idleness their condition will be worse than before. There is a certain logic to this reasoning, but it is a logic hard to swallow when one watches a . . . bucket-excavator . . . digging a ditch at a rate scores of men could not maintain. But what is the result when the machines sweep through an industry in a short time, replacing . . . fathers, sons and even grandsons . . . so that they simultaneously lose their livelihoods and all claim to status and standing? What happens to entire communities leveled by such traumas? What befalls the psyche and spirit of people so afflicted . . . ? [1]

Such questions have never burdened the consciences of coal companies, and have seldom disturbed the sympathy of politicians. A society dominantly industrial has no effective means either of democratizing the gains or of ameliorating the human costs of industrialization. The fate of workers is abandoned to "the market" and "the labor market."

Of the eastern Kentucky coal miners one needs to add that when they moved into the "coal camps" they left not only their homes but also the families, neighborhoods, and land-based household economies that had supported them at home. They thus became entirely dependent on the money economy and their wages. Once progress had taken away their wages, they became entirely dependent on "welfare," or they migrated in search of jobs to the cities, where again they were wage-dependent and now in circumstances for which their rural experience had in no way prepared them.

Similarly, when industrial machinery and chemicals came into the sugarcane and cotton lands of the South, the mostly black field hands and their families became immediately obsolete, useless and wageless, with no recourse but to take their chances in urban ghettos. They too had to move from rural homes, communities, and a land-based subsistence—in which, however poor, they had lived with a long-established competence—into situations alien to their experience and abilities.

Those who have been in this way uprooted, replaced and displaced, and who by their sufferings pay far more than their share of "the price of progress," are then subjected to versions of political regard dependent on the same social disconnection, and about equally irresponsible. The "conservatives," eagerly serving both God and Mammon, have concluded much to their convenience that the poor are poor or "jobless" because they are lazy, requiring only the incentive of starvation, or the starvation of their children, to become "productive members of society." The "liberals," serving an abstracted and oblique political compassion, assume that poverty and joblessness can somehow be corrected by the tiding over or new start supposedly granted by public charity and government "programs."

These attitudes issue from the great blank in the political-industrial mind that has forgotten, if it ever knew, the public and political value of securing for all citizens a reasonable permanence of dwelling place and vocation, which depends upon the widespread ownership of small farms and other economically supportive small properties. Lacking that fundamental connection, individuals, families, and neighborhoods can originate nothing in their own support, but become helplessly dependent on the money economy and the government, as now in fact we all are. Lacking that connection, the public economy becomes little more than a financial system irrelevant to economic life and to need, as ours now has done.

The following sentences speak as well as any I have ever read of the essentially democratic connection between people and land. The writer praises

> the spirit of independence which is generated in countries where the free cultivators of the soil constitute the major part of the population. It can scarcely be imagined how proudly man feels, however small his property may be, when he has a spot of arable land and pasture . . . [H]is independence being founded on permanent property, he has an interest in the welfare of the state, by supporting which he renders his own property more secure, and, although the value of the property may not be great, it is every day in his view . . . Those who wish to see only the two castes of capitalists and day-labourers, may smile at this union of independence and poverty.[2]

That statement is a part of Alexander Mackenzie's assessment of the "nineteenth-century clearances" of the small holders of the Scottish Highlands. It is a statement that Thomas

Jefferson would have recognized and honored. So would Virgil and several of the authors of the Bible. So would have my father and many other rural Kentuckians whose minds were formed a generation before World War II. They and many others spoke for an authentic, ancient human need to have and to belong to a piece of land, however small or poor, to live on and from, and to care for, a place offering a significant measure of life-support to themselves and their families and, as needed, to their neighbors. This is in no way like the land-greed of "them that join house to house, that lay field to field . . . that they may be placed alone in the midst of the earth!"[3]

The Scottish Highlanders who were "cleared" from their small holdings, to make way for landlords' sheep pastures and game preserves, were abandoned mostly to the choice between emigration and starvation. As I have already suggested, their fate was not unique. Such regardless harm was the deliberate result also of England's Enclosure Acts. The same dispossession of country people took place in Stalin's Russia, and is taking place now in China. The resemblance of these developments to our own clearances of the American Indians is plain enough. The modern American version, in addition to the casual substitution of machines for field hands, and also following World War II, was the semi-official agricultural policy of "too many farmers" or "Get big or get out." It was semi-official because no act of Congress gave it a legal basis. Its basis was the "expert" opinion of corporate, academic, and political leaders. The relatively self-sufficient producers on small farms, according to this opinion, needed to become members of the industrial "labor force" and consumers of industrial commodities. Reducing the number of farmers and farms became a devastatingly successful political goal. The "free market" was allowed to have its way, which meant, among much else, that the primary producers in the industrial food economy would buy dear and sell cheap. By now nearly all of the land-using population have left their farms and home places to be industrially or professionally employed, or unemployed, and to be entirely dependent on the ways and the products of industrialism. Or they have remained, as "farmers," to pilot enormous machines over thousands of acres continuously in annual row crops such as soybeans and corn.

From earliest times we have known, if we were willing to know, having learned by experience and example, that when people are disconnected from their land they suffer. But that is only half of the truth. The other half is that when its rightful people, the people who rightfully care for it, are absent from it, the land suffers. It is the mutual, indivisible suffering of land and people that sets in right perspective the suffering of either.

The first problem of a drastic reduction of the land-using population is to keep the land producing in the absence of the people. The expert solution followed unsurprisingly the expert doctrine of "too many farmers." At the end of World War II, the war industries conveniently could "gear up" to adapt the mechanical and chemical technologies of war to the "needs of agriculture." The departing farm families would be replaced by the re-rigged war technologies, depending upon a seemingly limitless bounty of "natural resources," mainly ores and fuels. Agriculture would become an industry. Farms would become factories, like other factories ever more automated and remotely controlled. Industrial land use thus has become a front in a war against the living world. For the remaining fewer and fewer farmers, this has required a shift of interest from husbanding the fertility of the land to the various means of consuming the fossil fuels—with consequences perhaps foreseeable even by the experts, had their eyes been open.

But there was a further problem that the experts did not recognize then, and have not recognized yet: Agricultural production without land maintenance can lead only to exhaustion. Land that is in use, if the use is to continue, must be used with care. And care is not, it can never be, an industrial product or an industrial result. It cannot be prescribed or enforced by a market, free or unfree. Care can come only from what we used to understand as the human heart, so called because it is central to human concerns and to human being. The human heart is informed by the history of care and by the need for it, also by the heritage of the skills of caring and of caretaking.

The replacement of our displaced farm families by technologies derived from warfare has involved, beyond appeal, a supposedly acceptable, and generally accepted, violence against land and people. By it we have established an analogy between land use and war that has remained remarkably consistent to our present wars with their transferable "precision" technologies of remote observation and control. The common theme is a terrible pragmatism that grants an absolute predominance of the end over the means, in oblivion or defiance of any natural or moral law that may stand in the way. In the industrial land economies, from agriculture to mining, anything coming from the land that cannot be sold is treated as an enemy, and this includes natural and human communities.

The quickest way is the best way: This is the industrial version of efficiency. The industrial economy thrives on the rapidest possible changes of technology and fashion. Industrial land use thrives, or its suppliers thrive, by ever-swifter passages of machines over the land. Anything obstructing or reducing speed must be cleared away. To realize this highest aim of industrial agriculture, everything must give way to the rule of the widest expanse and the straightest line. Every surviving woodland, every tree, every fencerow must be removed. So must the animals, their pastures and pens. So must the surplus people and their buildings. Streams must be straightened and ponds filled. Every acre that will support a tractor must be cropped. Such use of the land is determined entirely by the market, and is limited entirely by the capabilities of the available technology. Questions relating to ecological and human health, or to the health of the local economy, are easily ignored because there are no industrial answers to such questions.

The rhetoric and indignation of conservationists often leads to stereotyping and condemnation by category. I need now to be careful to avoid that. From the prevalence of villainous ways of land use, it does not necessarily follow that all industrial farmers and foresters are villains. For the sake of fairness and in the interest of valid remedies, we need to understand how economic systems and constraints, plus the availability of shortcutting technologies, incline or attract or force land users toward abuse. We need to understand how abuse is favored or rewarded in the absence of sound and conserving land-use policies, and of any informed public concern and discussion that might lead to such policies.

Moreover, though a large portion of our remnant of farmers are now fully industrialized and their "operations" more extensive than ever before, I believe that they have inherited the economic standing of farmers in general and nearly always. For reasons usually of scarcity or of crop failure elsewhere, some of them sometimes experience a good year or a few good years, but their future is never reasonably secure, and in the industrial era their children are less and less likely to become farmers. Though the corporations that supply "industrial inputs" to farmers and the corporations that purchase "farm products" may prosper exceedingly, the farmers themselves, the people who bear the primary financial burdens and who do the actual work, will be the last considered, the least respected, and the lowest paid.

And so however severe may be the current abuses of the land, and however urgent the need for conservation, we have got to bear in mind that the land will not be well used, because it cannot be, by people who cannot afford to use it well. I recently attended a meeting on agriculture and water quality, at which a thoughtful farmer made a point shockingly obvious. What he said ought, in reason, to have ended the meeting, though of course it did not. He said that keeping animal manure out of the streams makes sense, it makes both agricultural and economic sense, "but it is hard to think of your environmental responsibilities when you're wondering who will be the next family to live in your house."

To make as much sense as I can of our predicament, I must turn now to Wes Jackson's perception that for any parcel of land in human use there is an "eyes-to-acres ratio" that is right and necessary to save it from destruction. By "eyes" Wes means a competent watchfulness, aware of the nature and the history of the place, constantly present, always alert for signs of harm and signs of health. The necessary ratio of eyes to acres is not constant from one place to another, nor is it scientifically predictable or computable for any place, because from place to place there are too many natural and human variables. The need for the right eyes-to-acres ratio appears nonetheless to have the force of law.

Economic landscapes, in short, require the most careful watching. And "careful" is the right adjective here: People who don't care, or know enough to care, or care enough to know, don't watch. And here I need to add an indispensable comment from the biologist Robert B. Weeden, who read an earlier attempt at this essay:

> [T]he essential eye is both attentive and loving. I think you use the term caring, which can have the same meaning as loving. However, one may have a variety of motives for caring, including looking after an investment. The attentiveness needed is a whole and balanced thing, not allowed to skew over into mere analysis. Narrow focus is necessary but not sufficient. As to loving, it must never be left alone, at least in your context of relation to place. Romantics of the eighteenth and nineteenth centuries loved rural places, but as ideas and ideals—as projections of perfection. Someone has to check whether the lowing herd is chopping the life out of the saturated lea! [4]

What is necessary and attractive here is the introduction of the idea of a practical and practicing love. Reading Bob Weeden's letter caused me to think again of something I have, from my own experience, begun to know: how intimately related, how nearly synonymous, are the terms "love" and "know," how likely impossible it is to know authentically or well what one does not love, and how certainly impossible it is to love what one does not know.

To anybody who takes seriously the eyes-to-acres ratio, and

who is carefully and lovingly watching, it is apparent that the working landscapes of our country are now virtually deserted. In the vast, relatively flat acreages of the Midwest now given over exclusively to the production of corn and soybeans, the number of farmers is lower than it has ever been. I don't know what the average number of acres per farmer now is, but I do know that you often can drive for hours through those corn-and-bean deserts without seeing a human being beyond the road ditches, or any green plant other than corn and soybeans. Any people you may see at work, if you see any at work anywhere, almost certainly will be inside the temperature-controlled cabs of large tractors, the connection between the human organism and the soil organism perfectly interrupted by the machine. Thus we have transposed our culture, our cultural goal, of sedentary, indoor work to the fields. Some of the "field work" is now done by airplanes.

This contact, such as it is, between land and people is now brief and infrequent, occurring mainly at the times of planting and harvest. The speed and scale of this work have increased until it is impossible to give close attention to anything beyond the performance of the equipment. The condition of the crop of course is of concern and is observed, but not the condition of the land. And so the technological focus of industrial agriculture by which species diversity has been reduced to one or two crops, is reducing human participation ever nearer to zero. Under the preponderant rule of "labor-saving," the worker's attention to the work *place* has been effectively nullified even when the worker is present. The "farming" of corn-and-bean farmers—and of others as fully industrialized—has been brought down from the complex arts of tending or husbanding the land to the application of "purchased inputs" according to the instructions conveyed by labels and operators' manuals.

Almost suddenly in the last three years the Midwestern version of corn-and-bean farming has invaded the highly vulnerable sloping fields of my part of Kentucky—where the officially recommended and encouraged "no-till" farming, dependent upon herbicides, does not, as claimed, prevent erosion, and especially not under continuous cropping. (Until recently, weed control in crops was accomplished by plowing or other mechanical means of stirring and loosening the soil. The no-till method controls weeds, instead, by poisoning them with herbicides. Loosening the soil, of course, makes it vulnerable to erosion, the vulnerability increasing with the steepness of the land. The selling point that no-till stops erosion thus seems to justify planting on land that is too steep.) This expansion of the "cutting edge" has been caused by high grain prices, caused in turn by the officially recommended and encouraged production of "biofuels," supposedly sustainable but not so by ecological standards, and doubtfully so even economically.

We can suppose that the eyes-to-acres ratio is approximately correct when a place is thriving in human use and care. The sign of its thriving would be the evident good health and diversity, not just of its crops and livestock but also of its population of native and noncommercial creatures, including the community of creatures living in the soil. Equally indicative and necessary would be the signs of a thriving local and locally-adapted human economy.

The great and characteristic problem of industrial agriculture is that it does not distinguish one place from another. In effect, it blinds its practitioners to where they are. It cannot, by definition, be adapted to local ecosystems, topographies, soils, economies, problems, and needs.

The sightlessness and thoughtlessness of the imposition of the corn-and-bean industry upon the sloping or rolling countryside hereabouts is made vividly objectionable to me by my memory of the remarkably careful farming that was commonly practiced in these central Kentucky counties in the 1940s and 1950s—though, even then, amid much regardlessness and damage. The best farming here was then highly diversified in both plants and animals. Its basis was understood to be grass and grazing animals; cattle, sheep, hogs, and, during the 1940s, the workstock, all were pastured. Grain crops typically were raised to be fed; the farmers would say, "The grain raised here must *walk* off." And so in any year only a small fraction of the land would be plowed. I knew an excellent famer of that older kind who thought that only about 5 percent of most upland farms could be safely broken for row crops (best by rotating from sod and back to sod) in any year. This was farming fitted to the land, as J. Russell Smith said it should be.[5] And the commercial economy of the farms was augmented and supported by the elaborate subsistence economies of the households. "I may be sold out or run out," the farmers would say, "but I'll not be *starved* out."

My brother recently reminded me how carefully our father thought about the nature of our home countryside. He had witnessed the ultimate futility—the high costs to both farmer and farm—of raising corn for cash during the hard times of the 1920s and 1930s. He concluded, rightly, that the only crop that could be raised here both abundantly and profitably in the long run was grass. That was because we did not have large acreages that could safely be used for growing grain, but our land was aboundingly productive of grass, which moreover it produced more cheaply than any other crop. And the grass sod, which was perennial, covered and preserved the soil the year round.

A further indication of the quality of the farming here in the 1940s and 1950s, is that the Soil Conservation Service was more successful during those years than it would or could be again in the promotion of plowing and terracing on the contour to control soil erosion. Those measures at that time were permitted by the right scale of the farming and of the equipment then in use. Anybody familiar with topographic maps will know that contour lines, remaining strictly horizontal, over the irregularities of the land's surfaces, cannot be regularly spaced. This variability presents no significant problem to a farmer using one- or two-row equipment in relatively small lands or fields. And so for a while contour farming became an established practice on many farms, and to good effect. It was defeated primarily by the enlargement of fields and the introduction of larger equipment. Eventually many farmers simply ignored their terraces, plowing over them, the planted rows sometimes running straight downhill. Earlier a good many farmers had taken readily to the idea of soil conservation. A farmer in a neighboring county said, "I want the water to *walk* off my land, not run." But beyond a certain scale, the farming begins to conform to the demands of the machines, not to the nature of the land.

I should pause here to notice that within three paragraphs I have twice quoted farmers who used "walk" as an approving figure of speech: Grain leaving a farm hereabouts should *walk* off; and the rainwater fallen upon a farm should *walk*, not run. This is not accidental. The gait most congenial to agrarian thought and sensibility is walking. It is the gait best suited to paying attention, most conservative of land and equipment, and most permissive of stopping to look or think. Machines, companies, and politicians "run." Farmers studying their fields travel at a walk.

Farms that are highly diversified and rightly scaled tend, by their character and structure, toward conservation of the land, the human community, and the local economy. Such farms are both work places and homes to the families who inhabit them and who are intimately involved in the daily life of land

and household. Without such involvement, farmers cease to be country people and become in effect city people, industrial workers and consumers, living in the country.

To understand the complex and demanding requirements of good agriculture, and to know the vast acreage now given over to bad agriculture (leaving aside for now the vast acreage consigned to bad forestry), is to recognize the utter futility of the notion, apparently still prevalent among conservation groups, that the health of the natural world, revealingly called "the environment," can be preserved in parks and "wilderness areas." This drastic abbreviation of land stewardship permits no competent concern for the effects of the lowing herd upon the lea or of corn and beans upon the slopes. It holds that the gated communities of "the wild" will somehow preserve the natural health of "the planet."

Such conservationists, one imagines, might take instruction from scientists about the need for ecological health in the food-producing landscapes. But such scientists are rare and scattered. The predominant agricultural science of the universities, the corporations, and the government is still almost unanimously promoting industrial agriculture despite the by now overwhelming evidence of its failure: soil erosion, salinization, aquifer depletion, nutrient depletion, dependence on fossil fuels and toxic chemicals, pollution of streams and rivers, loss of genetic and ecological diversity, destruction of rural communities and the cultures of husbandry. The agricultural scientists and experts go doggedly on in their "cutting edge" rut because they either are employed by agribusiness or because their universities are now helplessly dependent on grants from agribusiness.

Urban conservationists, university scientists and intellectuals, journalists, powerful officials and politicians moreover are unlikely to live in the economic landscapes. In general they don't like the "boondocks" and the "nowheres" of rural America, and they don't know anything about them. Most of them know nothing of the issues of land use, and they think them unimportant. The sentimentalized ignorance of the romantic wilderness lovers, and the institutionalized, fear-enforced ignorance of agricultural scientists, are thus in turn permitted and supported by the ignorance of the general public, most of whom see the economic landscapes only through the windows of their speeding automobiles. If, by some rare chance, they should get out of their cars and walk in the fields, pastures, and woodlands, they most likely would take the present look of things to be "normal." Knowing no history of places, having no memories of them, they could not distinguish the country as it is from the country as it ever was. They would not recognize the signs of deterioration, or the numerous alien species that have come in as a side effect of global trade.

Nowhere is this ignorance more poignantly manifest than in the common use of words such as "land" and "ecosystem" simply as ideas or metaphors. I recently read *Ill Fares the Land*, a mostly admirable book, by Tony Judt, an admirable man. The book's title comes from a line in "The Deserted Village," Oliver Goldsmith's poem of protest against the Enclosure Acts. As Goldsmith used the word, "land" meant land. But Tony Judt's book never mentions the land. It speaks of "environmental well-being," of climate change and "environmental effects," it quotes John Maynard Keynes on "the beauty of the countryside," but its author clearly had not thought of the land itself, the land-use economies, or the natural world. To him "the land" is merely a figure of speech denoting "the nation" or "the national economy."[6]

In the absence of a widely practiced and capable attention to our use of the land, to the land-use economies, and to the natural sources of our life, we have a national, or global, economy consisting entirely of capital (rated at monetary value), minimal labor ("jobs," merely numbered, and the numbers always liable to reduction by technology), information (infinite perhaps, but never sufficient), marketing (seduction of the gullible), and consumption (conversion of goods into waste or poison). And so we have lost patriotism in the old sense of love for one's country, and have replaced it with an ignorant, hard-hearted military-industrial nationalism that devours the country.

Under such a dominance it is understandable that land use should be reduced to the application, at the greatest possible speed and with the least possible labor, of technology and information. Since no limit is implied in the economic assumptions of such use, its technology or its methods, its destructiveness is unlimited, far exceeding the reach of any envisionable public regulation or supervision, as in the mountaintop removal method of coal mining, which destroys absolutely and beyond remedy the original, invaluable forest ecosystem of the Appalachian coal fields. An economy operating on the basis merely of quantities runs oddly toward both infinity and nothing, limitless desire and final exhaustion. No billionaire, evidently, can be satisfied with one billion or with any conceivable number of billions. But the effect of so much wealth, uncontrollable because unaccountable and unknowable by any human mind, is to use up the world's real wealth, which is its ability to live and to renew its life.

I don't think we can set the terms of a restorative and conserving land-use economy simply by juggling and somehow fixing the technologies, methods, resources, assumptions, and regulations of the present economy. We seem to have exhausted the capacity of our present system to improve much of anything. Or it may be better to say that we improve things by means of costs that we never count or subtract from the supposed benefits, and so we relinquish any notion of net improvement, not to speak of net loss.

The possibility of actual improvement in our economic life, which is to say our way of living from our land, seems to lie, not just in stabilizing our occupation of our country on the basis of knowledgeable attachment to its localities, but also in studying the economic value of such intangible goods as knowledge, memory, familiarity, imagination, affection, sympathy, neighborliness, and so on. One might greatly lengthen this list simply by allowing the several goods to call forth their kindred, each of which, like the ones I have listed, would impose certain conditions and certain limits. An economy, of course, must deal in quantities, but an economy answerable to terms such as I have listed would be opposite, in its effects, to an economy merely of quantities. I resist the inclination to call such terms qualities or ideas, just as I resist the inclination to call them feelings. They certainly are informed by qualities, ideas, and feelings, but they also are mental powers capable of enforcing care in our treatment of persons, places, and things.

In thinking about the economy, not of agriculture or farming, but of a farm, we come quickly to see the value of knowledge. The knowledge of how to farm, how and when to do the work, has an obvious, and fairly reckonable, economic worth. But the knowledge that is limited to one's own particular farm—knowledge of its nature, character, history, limitations, and right use, gathered out of years of experience—also has an economic value that is far more specific and not so readily accounted. Its value can only be suggested by pointing out that it clearly is an asset to the farmer who has it, that it cannot be sold or adequately conveyed by instruction to a new owner, whose want of it will be an economic disadvantage requiring much time, and perhaps some costly mistakes, to remedy. The value of such knowledge may be further suggested by seeing that it is depreciated virtually to nothing by the continuous monocultures I have described.

The force and effect of such intangibles is nowhere better exemplified than in the better communities of the Amish, which, so far as my own observation goes, are the only communities in the United States that are successful by every appropriate standard. Some would argue that the fundamental power or principle of these communities is their religious faith, and some would argue, further, that no community can be successful without religious faith as a fundamental principle. I am inclined to accept their conclusion, though I doubt that it can be adequately demonstrated, let alone proved. And so I will deal here only with issues of economy—though, among the Amish, the economy is formed or informed at every point by religious faith.

I think it is reasonable to say that the fundamental principle of Amish economy is rightness of scale: rightness of the size of their farms, and the appropriateness of that size to the nature of the local landscape, to the community's way of farming, and to the scale of its work. Rightness of scale gives scope and efficacy to the powers I have listed, and to others. It is the principle that allows diversity, flexibility, and local adaptation of farm enterprises.

Amish economy is an economy dependent upon limits strictly understood and observed. And each of the limits produces an economic advantage. Traction for field work, for example, is limited to the use of horses or mules. And that limit implies a limit of farm size; it implies diversity, which implies a structure of interdependent and mutually supportive plant and animal enterprises; it makes the farm the source of most of its operating energy and fertility—all of which, together, lower the cost of production.

Another limit, of almost incalculable significance, is neighborliness. This means that you would rather have a neighbor than to have your neighbor's farm, and here is another limitation on the size of farms. If their farms are of the right size, neighbors can help one another in times of trouble or when the work calls for many hands. If one has a neighbor—in the sense derived from the Gospels, as it is here—then one has help, and help is an economic advantage. If neighbors exchange work, they don't have to hire help and pay in cash.

The Amish famously, or infamously, limit formal schooling to eight grades. (This is not at all to say that they limit learning. Some Amishmen, for example, have gone on to learn mechanical engineering.) They limit schooling in order to keep their children in the community. This makes sense if you *want* to keep your children in the community, and if you have understood that the purpose of mainstream education is to prepare children, and especially country children, to *leave* the community. If you contrive in general to keep the community's children in the community, there are two desirable results: 1) The children, from earliest childhood, learn the community's work, by observing it and, as they become able, by doing it; and 2) If you keep all or most of the community's children in the community, then as a matter of course you keep the brightest and most talented ones. To keep the community's own brightest and most talented members in the community, in the community's local circumstances, doing the community's work, is to have the best intelligence and talent applied to that work, producing good examples that can be followed by neighbors. This is an economic advantage. Moreover, the community may thus gain the competence to deal with tools, to quote again my friend Robert B. Weeden, "that take more skill not to use, than to use."[7]

If on a farm of a conscientiously limited size you balance row crops and forages with an appropriate number of animals, then as a matter of course you become familiar with those animals. You can know them individually, and so sympathy can enter into your association with them. The best-known example of this is Psalm 23, a shepherd's psalm in which the shepherd, identifying himself as one of God's sheep, identifies profoundly with his own sheep: "He maketh *me* to lie down in green pastures: he leadeth *me* beside the still waters" [my emphases].

Just so, if by the same order of limitation you use a team of horses for field work, you know by sympathy, by imagining yourself "in their place," when they are overheating or over-tired or when you are asking too much. From there it is not far to sympathy for the field you are working in, which also can be too much demanded upon, can be overworked and in need of rest. Imagination leads to sympathy, sympathy leads to good care, and all three convey economic advantages.

Once this pattern of interdepending limits and advantages has been understood, it can be described perhaps endlessly. But I have said enough to show why, if you drive through one of the good Amish communities, you will see a lot of people outdoors and busy. You will see that they have honored their places with the visible signs of good work lovingly done. And you will think again, with sharpened sadness, of the nearly always deserted "farms" of thousands of acres of corn and beans.

II.

I have spoken so far of the decline of country work, but the decline of country pleasures is at least equally significant. If the people who live and work in the country don't also enjoy the country, a valuable and necessary part of life is missing. And for families on farms of a size permitting them to be intimately lived on and from, the economic life of the place is itself the primary country pleasure. As one would expect, not every day or every task can be a pleasure, but for farmers who love their livestock there is pleasure in watching the animals graze and in winter feeding. There is pleasure in the work of maintenance, the redemption of things worn or broken, that must go on almost continuously. There is pleasure in the growing, preserving, cooking, and eating of the good food that the family's own land provides. But around this core of the life and work of the farm are clustered other pleasures, in their way also life-sustaining, and most of which are cheap or free.

I live in a country that would be accurately described as small-featured. There are no monumental land forms, no peaks or cliffs or high waterfalls, no wide or distant vistas. Though it is by nature a land of considerable beauty, there is little here that would attract vacationing wilderness lovers. It is blessed by a shortage of picturesque scenery and mineable minerals. The topography, except in the valley bottoms, is rolling or sloping. Along the sides of the valleys, the slopes are steep. It is divided by many hollows and streams, and it has always been at least partly wooded.

Because of the brokenness and diversity of the landscape, there was never until lately a clean separation here between the pursuits of farming and those of hunting and gathering. On many farms the agricultural income, including the home-grown and homemade subsistence of the households, would be supplemented by hunting or fishing or trapping or gathering provender from the woods and berry patches—perhaps by all of these. And beyond their economic contribution, these activities were forms of pleasure. Many farmers kept hounds or bird dogs. The gear and skills of hunting and fishing belonged to ordinary daily and seasonal life. More ordinary was the rambling about and looking that kept people aware of the condition of the ground, the crops, the pastures, and the livestock, of the state of things in the house yard and the garden, in the woods, and along the sides of the streams.

My own community, centered upon the small village of Port Royal, is along the Kentucky River and in the watersheds of local tributaries. Its old life, before the industrialization of much of the farmland and the urbanization of the people, was under the influence of the river, as other country communities of that time were under the influence of the railroads. In the neighborhood of Port Royal practically every man and boy, some girls and women too, fished from time to time in the Kentucky River. Some of the men fished "all the time" or "way too much." Until about a generation ago, there was some commercial fishing. And I can remember when hardly a summer day would pass when, from the house where eventually I would live, you could not hear the shouts of boys swimming in the river, often flying out into the water from the end of a swinging rope. I remember when I was one of them. My mother, whose native place this was, loved her girlhood memories of swimming parties and picnics at the river. In hot weather she and her friends would walk the mile from Port Royal down to the river for a cooling swim, and then would make the hot walk back up the hill to town.

Now all of that belongs to the past. The last of the habituated fishermen of the local waters are dead. They have been replaced by fishermen using expensive "bassboats," almost as fast as automobiles. This sport is less describable as "fishing" than as "using equipment." In the last year only one man, comparatively a newcomer, has come to the old landing where I live to fish with trotlines—and, because of the lack of competition, he has caught several outsize catfish. Some local people, and a good many outsiders, hunt turkeys and deer. There is still a fair amount of squirrel hunting. The bobwhite, the legendary gamebird of this region, is almost extinct here, and the bird hunters with them. A rare few still hunt with hounds.

Most remarkable is the disappearance of nearly all children and teenagers from the countryside, and in general from the out-of-doors. The technologies of large-scale industrial agriculture are too complicated and too dangerous to allow the participation of children. For most families around here, the time is long gone when children learned to do farmwork by playing at it, and then taking part in it, in the company of their parents. It seems that most children now don't play much in their house yards, let alone in the woods and along the creeks. Many now descend from their school buses at the ends of lanes and driveways to be carried the rest of the way to their houses in parental automobiles. Most teenagers apparently divide their out-of-school time between indoor entertainment and travel in motor vehicles. The big boys no longer fish or swim or hunt or camp out. Or work. The town boys, who used to hire themselves out for seasonal or part-time work on the farms, no longer find such work available, or they don't wish to do the work that is available.

Not so long ago, talking with one of my contemporaries about the time before school consolidation, when there were five high schools in Henry County, I said, "When we were boys, there were five basketball teams in this county."

He said, "I'll tell you something else. In my senior year, any of the five could have beaten this one we've got now."

"Well, you all were in shape," I said.

"Yes," he said. "We *worked*."

More recently I heard a woman complaining that her husband could not hire anybody to help him with farmwork, "not even young people."

Somebody asked, "What *are* the young people doing?"

She was indignant: "Nothing!"

They aren't doing nothing, of course, but nothing might be preferable to what they are likely to be doing. For young people accustomed (by habit and indoctrination) to indoor life, the dominant attractions are drugs (including alcohol), sex, and various digital devices. The drug use is merely predictable in a society in which drugs are everywhere recommended for every imaginable discomfort and "need." Sex (arranged by telecommunication, using various digital devices) is promoted everywhere as another cure-all, as an incentive to participate in the economy of spending and consuming, and no doubt as another of our new crop of "rights." The digital devices are recommended or required in order to prepare the young for "the world of the future." The cost of this expensive preparation is virtual exile from the present world that is available at no cost outside their front doors. And so they spend their liveliest years mostly sitting and looking at screens.

Local people who regularly hunted or fished or foraged or walked or played in the local countryside served the local economy and stewardship as inspectors, rememberers, and story tellers. They gave their own kind of service to the eyes-to-acres ratio. Now most of those people are gone or absent, along with most of the farming people who used to be at work here.

With them have gone the local stories and songs. When people begin to replace stories from local memory with stories from television screens, another vital part of life is lost. I have my own memories of the survival in a small rural community of its own stories. By telling and retelling those stories, people told themselves who they were, where they were, and what they had done. They thus maintained in ordinary conversation their own living history. And I have from my neighbor, John Harrod, a thorough student of Kentucky's traditional fiddle music, his testimony that every rural community once heard, sang, and danced to at least a few tunes that were uniquely its own. What is the economic value of stories and songs? What is the economic value of the lived and living life of a community? My argument here is directed by my belief that the art and the life of settled rural communities are necessary to the sustainability of a life-supporting economy. But their value is incalculable. It can only be acknowledged and respected, and our present economy is incapable, and cannot on its own terms be made capable, of such acknowledgement and respect.

Meanwhile, the farmlands and woodlands of this neighborhood are being hurt worse and faster by bad farming and bad logging than at any other time in my memory. The signs of this abuse are often visible even from the roads, but nobody is looking. Or to people who are looking, but seeing from no perspective of memory or knowledge, the country simply looks "normal." Outsiders who come visiting almost always speak of it as "beautiful." But along this river, the Kentucky, which I have known all my life and have lived beside for half a century, there is a large and regrettable recent change, clearly apparent to me, and to me indicative of a drastic change in water quality, but perfectly invisible to nearly everybody else.

I don't remember what year it was when I first noticed the disappearance of the native black willows from the low-water line of this river. Their absence was sufficiently noticeable, for the willows were both visually prominent and vital to the good health of the river. Wherever the banks were broken by "slips" or the uprooting of large trees, and so exposed to sunlight, the willows would come in quickly to stabilize the banks. Their bushy growth and pretty foliage gave the shores of the river a distinctive grace, now gone and much missed by the few who remember. Like most people, I don't welcome bad news, and so I said to myself that perhaps the willows were absent only from the stretch of the river that I see from my house and work places. But in 2002 for the first time in many years I had the use of a motorboat, and I examined carefully the shores of the twenty-seven-mile pool between locks one and two. I saw a few old willows at the tops of the high banks, but none at or near the low-water line, and no young ones anywhere.

The willows still live as usual along other streams in the area, and they thrive along the shore of the Ohio River just above the mouth of the Kentucky at Carrollton. The necessary conclusion is that their absence from the Kentucky River must be attributable to something seriously wrong with the water. And so, since 2002, I have asked everybody I met who might be supposed to know: "Why have the black willows disappeared from the Kentucky River?" I have put this question to conservationists, to conservation organizations specifically concerned with the Kentucky River, to water-quality officials and to university biologists. And I have found nobody who could tell me why. Except for a few old fishermen, I have found nobody who knew they were gone.

This may seem astonishing. At least, for a while, it astonished me. I thought that in a state in which water pollution is a permanent issue, people interested in water quality surely would be alert to the disappearance of a prominent member of the riparian community of a major river. But finally I saw that such ignorance is more understandable than I had thought.

A generation or so ago, when fishing and the condition of the river were primary topics of conversation in Port Royal, the disappearance of the willows certainly would have been noticed. Fishermen used to tie their trotlines to the willows. That time, as I've said, is past, and I was seeking local knowledge from conservationists and experts and expert conservationists. But most conservationists, like most people now, are city people. They "escape" their urban circumstances and preoccupations by going on vacations. They thus go into the countryside only occasionally, and their vacations are unlikely to take them into the economic landscapes. They want to go to parks, wilderness areas, or other famous "destinations." Government and university scientists often have economic concerns or responsibilities, and some of them do venture into farmland or working forests or onto streams and rivers that are not "wild." But it seems they are not likely to have a particular or personal or long-term interest in such places, or to go back to them repeatedly and often over a long time, or to maintain an economic or recreational connection to them. Such scientists affect the eyes-to-acres ratio probably less than the industrial farmers.

It seems to me significant, and not a bit surprising, that among the many conservationists I have encountered in my home state, the most competent witness by far is Barth Johnson, a retired game warden who is a dedicated trapper, hunter, and fisherman, as he has been all his life. Barth has devoted much of his life to conservation. Like most conservationists he is informed about issues and problems. Unlike most, he is exceptionally alert to what is happening in the actual countryside that needs to be conserved. This is because he is connected to the neighboring fields and woods and waters by bonds of economy and pleasure, both at once. Because those bonds are long-sustained and continued from year to year, he knows those places well. He has, as a matter of course, a year-round interest in the health—which is, in the best sense, the productivity—of the countryside. Moreover, he has lived for thirty years in the same place at the lower end of the Licking River. This greatly increases the value of his knowledge, for he can speak of changes *over time*. People who stay put and remain attentive know that the countryside changes, as it must, and for better or worse.

In his grasp of ecological principles, Barth is completely up with the times, and in some ways maybe ahead of the times, but he also is genuinely a countryman of a kind that is old and now rare. As opposed to writers, the best story *tellers* are people who spend a lot of time outdoors. Barth is well supplied with stories, most of them funny, all of them interesting, but some of them could be better classed as "reports."

He tells a story about Harris Creek, a small stream along which he had trapped for many years. It was richly productive, and Barth was careful never to ask too much of it. But in 2007, confident that it would be as it always had been, he went there with his traps and discovered that the stream was dead. He could not find a live minnow or crawfish. There were no animal tracks. So far as he could tell, there could be only one reason for this: In the spring of that year, the bottom-land along the creek had been herbicided in preparation for a seeding of alfalfa. In 2008, the stream was still dead. In 2009, there was "a little coon activity." Finally, in 2013, the stream was "close to normal."

I have also learned from Barth that upstream as far as he has looked, to a point two and a half miles above the small town of Boston, the black willows are gone from the Licking River. And in October 2013, he wrote me that the river had turned a brownish "brine" color that he had never seen before.

What happened to the willows? Two young biologists at Northern Kentucky University are now at work on the question, and perhaps they will find the answer. But other scientists have led me to consider the possibility that such questions may never be answered. It may be extremely difficult or impossible to attach a specific effect to a specific cause in a large volume of flowing water.

What killed Harris Creek? Barth's evidence is "anecdotal," without scientifically respectable proof. I have read scientific papers establishing that the herbicide glyphosate and its "degradation products" are present in high concentrations in some Mississippi River tributaries, but the papers say nothing about the effects. I have called up scientists working on water quality, including one of the authors of one of the papers on glyphosate. What about the *effects*? Good question. Nobody knows the answer. It seems that the research projects and the researchers are widely scattered, making such work somewhat incoherent. And besides there is always the difficulty of pinning a specific cause to a specific effect. To two of these completely friendly and obliging people I told Barth's story of Harris Creek: Does that surprise you? One said it did not surprise him. The other said it was possible but unlikely that the stream was killed by an herbicide. Was an insecticide also involved?

What caused the strange discoloration of the Licking River? Since the discoloration was visible until obscured by mud in the water when the river rose, I suppose that, if it happens again, the odd color could be traced upstream to a source.* Will somebody do that? I don't know. Is any scientist from any official body monitoring the chemical runoff from croplands and other likely sources? I have been asking that question too, and so far I have asked nobody who could answer.

In my search for answers, it may be that I have been making a characteristic modern mistake of relying on experts, which

---

* As of July 2014, it has not happened again.

has revealed a characteristic modern failure: Experts often don't know and sometimes can never know. Beneficiaries of higher education, of whom I am one, often give too much credit to credentials.

By now, my interest has necessarily shifted from an attempt to find answers to an attempt to understand the implications, not just of my failure so far to find answers, but of my failure so far to find any reason to think that answers are likely to be found. And so I must back up to what I do actually know and start again.

I know that the willows have disappeared, apparently because of some toxic chemical in the water. And I know that this is the result of a scientific success in developing a chemical that serves some industrial purpose, but with water pollution as a side effect. It is also the result of a scientific failure to notice—or to care, if noticed—that this chemical has "accidentally" polluted the river.

The countryside and its waterways are now being significantly, recognizably, and sometimes measurably damaged by industrialized science. Because of scientific success and scientific failure, toxic chemicals are on the loose, the effects of which the available science does not know and therefore cannot hope to remedy. This obviously is beyond the competence of people who are not scientists. If anybody now is going to maintain an effective vigilance over the runoff of toxic chemicals from crop monocultures or surface mines or other industrial sites, that vigilance will have to be maintained by scientists (such as they are). But there is no indication that there is enough money anywhere to hire enough scientists to do this. And how could enough scientists be found to watch carefully enough over such an extent of country and so many miles of creeks and rivers?

To be fair, there are a lot of amateurs who voluntarily watch over some of our waterways, and some of these people become competent at testing for the presence of pollutants. But such vigilance, to be effective, must be constant and sustained over a long time, and I am unsure of the extent to which this has been, or can be, achieved. The problem is the "mobility" of our people, which obviously limits their ability to pay attention to places.

In the middle of the last century we had within easy reach the possibility of preserving a right ratio of eyes to acres. From people and ways then in place, we could have cultivated, educated, and encouraged a population of vigilant land stewards attached to our economic landscapes by bonds of economy, pleasure, affection, and long memory, possessing the cultural means and imperatives of good care. We not only abandoned that possibility but condemned it as of no worth, substituting a program of industrial innovation, scientific responsibility, and governmental regulation that appears definitively to have failed. Of the "spill" of 4-methylcyclohexane methanol that contaminated the water supply of 300,000 West Virginians, a *New York Times* editorial noticed that this was "the third major chemical accident in the region in five years," adding that "the EPA has tested just 200 of the roughly 85,000 chemicals in use today." The *Times* editors called for "meaningful reform."[8] But by what conceivable reform could any agency locate, in all their inevitable wanderings, transformations, and combinations, and make harmless 85,000 chemicals already in use?

As another example, the Water Quality Branch of the Kentucky state government's Division of Water has nine biologists to monitor the state's 92,000 surface miles of streams. That is a biologist-to-miles ratio of 1 to more than 10,000. What, one has to ask, can be the adequacy of one biologist per 10,000 miles of streams? Or: What would be the value of one biologist per 10,000 miles compared to the value of one vigilant and stewardly farmer or trapper every 10 or even 100 miles—with, let us say, a staff of public biologists to help when there is a question or a problem?

Confronting industrial agriculture in particular, we are requiring ourselves to substitute science for citizenship, community membership, and land stewardship. But science fails at all of these. Science as it now predominantly is, by definition and on its own terms, does not make itself accountable for unintended effects. The intended effect of chemical nitrogen fertilizer, for example, is to grow corn, whereas its known effect on the Mississippi River and the Gulf of Mexico is a catastrophic accident. Moreover science of this kind is invariably limited and controlled by the corporations that pay for it.

In the economic landscapes, now so desperately in want of proper stewards and so little watched over, the industrial economy is free to do anything it can do, according to its wishes. This is a triumph of laissez-faire economics riding upon a triumph of its laissez-faire science—a science free to invent causes, and free of worry about effects. This triumph, highly complicated, highly profitable to a few corporations, intelligible (somewhat) only to experts, is nevertheless limited by its dependence on exhaustible materials, including, as now used, the soil. The bad ecological effects, even more complicated, and as now "regulated," may be limitable only by disease and death. This is the industrial version of the human predicament.

To this the only rational response is that it has been a mistake to allow industrialism, from the beginning, to measure its conduct exclusively by its own success, using such standards as mechanical efficiency or monetary profit, and ignoring all else. This great project of continuous technical innovation and obsolescence, substituting technologies for human workers, was intentionally wrong from the start in its evasion of the long-established moral requirement of neighborliness. Its ecological, and therefore its long-term economic, wrongs may at first have been to some degree innocent, for the earliest industrial abuses of nature were comparatively slight. No doubt the availability of long-distance transportation from "remote" areas encouraged the assumption that the world's supply of raw materials was all but infinite. And the availability in North America of "new land" to the west for three hundred years encouraged, and more or less subsidized, land abuses in the east. Now, though it certainly is possible to know better, and many people do, most industrialists still have not learned better. The frontier superstitions of the inexhaustibility of natural supplies and of the adequacy of human concern still prevail in the face of the overwhelming evidence against them.

Our original and continuing mistake has been to ignore the probability, even the inevitability, of a formal misfitting between the human economy and the economy of nature, or between economy and ecology. This misfitting has been dangerous and damaging at least since the beginnings of agriculture. The reason for this is the limited competence of the human mind, which will never fully comprehend the forms and functions of the natural world. With the development of industrialism, this misfitting has become increasingly a contradiction or opposition between industrial technologies and the creatures of nature, tending always toward the destruction of creatures, creaturely habitat, and creaturely life. We can respond rationally to this predicament only by honest worry, unrelenting caution, and propriety of scale. We must not put too much, let alone everything, at risk. We must never tolerate permanent damage to the ecosphere or to any of its parts. We must not, because we cannot for very long, tolerate compromises with soil erosion and agricultural poisons.

It is anyhow clear that if we want to do better, we will have to recognize the old mistake as a mistake: no more euphemisms such as "creative destruction," no more "sacrificing" of a present good for "greater good in the future." We will have to repudiate the too-simple industrial standards and replace them with the comprehensive standard of ecological health, realizing that this standard involves necessarily the humane obligation of neighborliness both to other humans and to other creatures. This means that all our uses of the natural world must be governed by our willingness to learn the nature of every place, and to submit to nature's limits and requirements for the use of every place. In short, agriculture and forestry must finally submit to ecology. Mining of course is not natural by any stretch of the term. Unlike agriculture and forestry, it cannot be made analogous to natural processes, because by method and purpose it exhausts its sources. But, at least, it must no longer be allowed to extract wealth from under the ground by destroying the invariably greater, self-renewing wealth that is on the surface. The human economy must operate, to the always extendable limits of its ability, as a good neighbor in both the natural and the human communities, because in the long run the health of one is the health of the other.

The history of industrialism has been an ever-ramifying series of substitutions. It began and has continued by substitutions of two kinds: the substitution of hotter to hottest fuels for the cooler energies of gravity, sunlight, wind, and food; and the substitution of ever more "sophisticated" technologies for human work and care.

The side effects of our use of fossil and nuclear fuels are too infamous to require much notice here. Their extraction has been increasingly, and often irreparably, damaging to the ecosphere, as well as to human communities and workers. Their use produces enormous volumes of earthborne and airborne poisons that human intelligence has never learned what to do with, probably because the safe disposal of permanently dangerous substances cannot be learned. The farce of such "disposability" is a major theme of the history of industrialism.

Another major theme is the disposability of people, and this is not a farce. It is one of the versions of "creative destruction," which is to say the theme of heartlessness, heartbreak, and permanent damage to people and their communities, endlessly repeated from the beginning, and with no proposed or theoretical end. We now use "Luddite" as a term of contempt, and this usage, often by people who consider themselves compassionate and humane, implies a sort of progressivist etiquette by which, in the interest of the future (of the more fortunate), we are to submit passively to our obsolescence, disemployment, displacement, and (likely enough) impoverishment. We smear this over with talk of social mobility, upward mobility, and retraining, but this is as false and cynical as the association of "safe" with the extraction, transportation, and use of fossil and nuclear fuels. Customarily we ignore the possibility that people's knowledge, intelligence, and skills may be needed in the places where their minds were formed, also the likelihood that such assets will become worthless as soon as the people leave home. We seem to have overlooked as well the possibility of using technologies to ameliorate the working conditions and the lives of workers while keeping them in place. Coal companies, for example, readily have used the newest technology to speed and cheapen the extraction of coal, but they often have used it reluctantly or too late to provide for the health and safety of their employees.

Replacement of workers by machines becomes more serious when it is enabled by the degradation of work. We have ignored the limits of compatibility between labor-saving and good work. And we have degraded almost all work by reducing the generously qualitative idea of "vocation" or "calling" to the merely quantitative integer, "a job." The purpose of education now is to make everybody eligible for "a job." A primary function of politics is "job creation." Persons deprived of work that they have loved and enjoyed and performed with pride are to consider their loss well-remedied by some form of "welfare" or "another job."

The idea of vocation attaches to work a cluster of other ideas, including devotion, skill, pride, pleasure, the good stewardship of means and materials. Here we have returned to intangibles of economic value. When they are subtracted, what remains is "a job," always implying that work is something good only to escape: "Thank God it's Friday." "A job" pretty much equals bad work, which can be performed as well or better by a machine. Once the scale and speed of farmwork have overridden any care for the health of the land community and any pride in the beauty of the farm, then we can talk, as we now are talking, of farming by remote control.

If such substitutions appear to work, we must consider the likelihood that they work only temporarily or according to criteria that are too simple or false. And we must acknowledge that some do not work at all: A "service economy" is immediately a falsehood when it is staffed by phone-answering robots. The computerization and robotification of the United States Postal "Service," far from improving the service, has impaired its ability to transport and deliver the mail on time or at any time. Somewhere along the line of industrial substitutions, it appears certain that we will find ourselves again confined within, and sharing the fate of, the natural, naturally-limited, industrially-depleted world that we have thought to transcend by more and more engineering. And then we will know, needing no experts to tell us, that our world, like our bodies, cannot survive unstanched bleeding and repeated doses of poison.

To replace industrial standards by the standard of ecological health would undo a failed substitution. It would not undo the history and the legacy of industrialism. We are not going to have the privilege of a clean slate or a new start. A change of standards would certainly change our ways of living and working, but those changes, even as they are chosen or forced upon us, cannot come with the speed of our various technological revolutions. They will require more patience than haste. (It may be that we can keep without harm some industrial comforts: warm baths in wintertime maybe, maybe painless dentistry).

Though a clean slate is impossible, as it has always been, we are not destitute of instructions and examples. Though our present anxieties incline us toward theories and illustrations of the natural rapaciousness of humans, not all humans and not all human communities have been so. I don't think the present bunch of living humans can be allowed to make the (very restful) claim that there is nothing they can do, pleading the incorrigibility of their nature or their circumstances. And so I will end this essay with an inventory of the resources we have at hand that will support us in our effort to do better. This is *an* inventory, not *the* inventory. My obligation here is only to show that we do have resources, probably enough, if we would pay attention to them.

1 – First and fundamental are the examples of nature's own ways of land care in the native ecosystems that precede the human economy, also in some humanly modified ecosystems that preceded the industrial economy. These ways have been carefully studied by agricultural scientists from Albert Howard, Aldo Leopold, and others before the middle of the last century to Wes Jackson and his colleagues at The Land Institute in Kansas right now. One of our most urgent needs

is for ecologists, trained in the native forests and prairies, to apply their knowledge in the economic landscapes. We humans, because of our limited intelligence, are never going to understand perfectly the nature of any place, or fit our local economies perfectly into local ecosystems. But the right instructions, or the right "model," for our use of a place can come only from the nature of the place.

2 – We have from all over the world, from F. H. King's *Farmers of Forty Centuries*, 1911, to the ongoing work of Vandana Shiva, examples of long-enduring traditional or peasant agricultures. These seem to have come from respectful and competent observation of the nature of places, and they have embodied natural processes or analogues thereof.

3 – We have Thomas Jefferson's great principle: "The small landholders are the most precious part of a state."9 If we understand that the state and the state's economy depend upon the land, and if we understand the numerousness, diversity, uniqueness, and vulnerability of the land's small places, and so their dependence upon human care, we cannot doubt the truth of Jefferson's rule.

4 – Scattered about the country, and concentrated in some Amish communities, we have, still surviving, farmers and foresters who have held to established good practices and tried

for better. It is not altogether a secret that in many a rural community you will find farmers or memories of farmers who have survived, even prospered, in hard times by limiting their farms to a manageable size, by taking care of them, by avoiding or minimizing debt, by limiting or avoiding purchases of new equipment, by subsisting so far as possible from their own land, and in general by saving rather than spending.

5 – Over the last two or three decades, there has been a growing national and international movement toward local economies, starting with economies of local food. This has been little noticed and poorly understood by the news media, mostly ignored in the state capitals and in Washington, D.C. Some city and county governments, however, have taken notice of this movement and understood its importance. For example, the local food effort is now well established as a part of the economic development plan of Louisville, Kentucky. To bring a local demand and a local supply into existence more or less simultaneously and on the principle of cooperation is a task obviously difficult, complicated, and long. But it has begun (there are now many examples in many places), and from nothing only a few years ago it has come a remarkable distance, though the distance ahead is much longer. This project involves food production *in* cities as well as around them, and it is fostering a necessary urban agrarianism among gardeners and consumers.

6 – We have a fairly long history of organic farming and gardening. We need to say, I think, that organic is as organic does. The term has often been too negatively defined (You *don't* use chemicals), and it can be too loosely defined, but it has always implied the standard of good health, and it seems by now to have escaped its old shadow of kookiness.

7 – For half a dozen years we have had the 50-Year Farm Bill, which addresses the specifically agricultural problems of soil erosion, toxicity, loss of diversity, and the destruction of rural communities. It proposes to invert the ratio of 80 percent annual and 20 percent perennial crops at present to 20 percent annual and 80 percent perennial crops in fifty years. This bill certainly comes from beyond the present margin of farm policy, and of course the habitual objectors are happy to point out that there is at present no chance of its passage. But such a farsighted bill could not have been written by people foolish enough to believe in its immediate passage.

8 – The 50-Year Farm Bill was published in 2009 by The Land Institute in Salina, Kansas, with the concurrence of other farm and conservation groups all over the country. That it came from The Land Institute should be no surprise, for that organization's great project for nearly forty years has been the perennialization of agriculture, arriving finally at perennial grainfields of mixed species, in analogy to the native prairie. This project of perennial grain crops has now spread

from Kansas to other states and other countries. The first of the necessary medley of perennial grains, a domesticated intermediate wheatgrass, is already well developed and may be ready for distribution to farmers in eight to ten years. That in itself is a remarkable achievement, though much remains to be done. But I want to suggest that the kind of science practiced at The Land Institute is itself a great and necessary resource. It is by definition a local science, carried on conscientiously in the contexts of the local ecosystem and the local human community. Whatever is developed in that place will require local adaptation, and the careful employment of many minds in other places. This science, moreover, is carried on with respect for local nature and local humanity. It is not going to produce a poison or an explosive.

9 – This is somewhat speculative, since I am not an economist or an accountant, but I believe that our present systems of economy and accounting can be greatly and usefully improved simply by becoming more inclusive and more honest. My impression is that the prominent economists who advise and influence the government pay little attention to the so-called economy's basis in nature or to the use and produce of the land. The ruling assumption seems to be that a thriving economy can be sustained by abuse of the land and of the people who do the land's work. I remember, of course, my argument that some things of real economic worth cannot be quantified and accounted. But there should be a full and fair

accounting of things that are accountable. Many of the costs of water pollution, for example, can be determined, and those costs should be charged to water-polluting industries and their customers. We need to be less interested in the "growth" of our gross income, and more interested in the subtraction of real costs and in net benefits.

10 – Finally, and most necessarily, we have the ancient and long-enduring cultural imperative of neighborly love and work. This becomes ever more important as hardly imaginable suffering is imposed upon all creatures by industrial tools and industrial weapons. If we are to continue, in our only world, with any hope of thriving in it, we will have to expect neighborly behavior of sciences, of industries, and of governments, just as we expect it of our citizens in their neighborhoods.

NOTES

1. Henry Caudill, *The Watches of the Night* (Ashland, Kentucky: The Jesse Stuart Foundation, 2010; originally published by Little Brown, 1979), 268–69.

2. Alexander Mackenzie, *The Highland Clearances* (Glasgow: Alexander Maclaren, 1966), 43–44.

3. Isaiah 5:8

4. Robert B. Weeden, personal letter, January 23, 2013.

5. J. Russell Smith, *Tree Crops* (New York: Harcourt, Brace and Company, 1929), 260.

6. Tony Judt, *Ill Fares the Land* (New York: Penguin, 2010).

7. Robert B. Weeden, "Small Forays into Big Spaces" (unpublished essay).

8. *New York Times*, January 17, 2014, A20.

9. Thomas Jefferson, *Writings* (New York: Library of America, 1984), 842.

9

For the 50-Year
Farm Bill

[2012]

1 – The uplands of my home country in north central Kentucky are sloping and easily eroded, dependent for safekeeping upon year-round cover of perennial plants. Its best agricultural use is for the production of grazing animals, most of the land in pastures and hayfields, and perhaps 5 to 10 percent plowed and row-cropped in any year. This was the practice of the best farmers in this part of the country fifty or sixty years ago.

II – The land husbandry here, as elsewhere, has been in decline since the end of World War II, as agriculture has become more and more industrial, and more and more of the farming people have taken urban jobs or moved away.

III – But recently and almost suddenly, as ethanol production has driven up the price of grain, our fragile uplands have been invaded by corn and soybeans. Whole farms, with sloping fields that have been in grass as long as I can remember, have been herbicided and planted to annual crops that, because of the drastic reduction of the number of farmers, will not be protected in winter by fall-sown cover crops.

IV – This is agriculture determined entirely by the market, and limited only by the capacities of machines and chemicals. Its entirely predictable ruination is the result of degenerate science and the collapse of local farming cultures.

V – Industrial agriculture characteristically proceeds by single solutions to single problems: If you want the most money from your land *this year*, grow the crops for which the market price is highest. Though the ground is sloping, kill the standing vegetation and use a no-till planter. For weed control, plant an herbicide-resistant crop variety and use more herbicide.

VI – But even officially approved industrial technologies do not alter reality. The supposed soil-saving of no-till farming applies to annual crops during the growing season, but the weather continues through the fall and winter and early spring. Rain continues. Snow falls. The ground freezes and thaws. A dead sod or dead weeds or the dead residue of annual crops is not an adequate ground cover. If this usage continues year after year on sloping land, and especially following soybeans, the soil will erode; it will do so increasingly. And this will be erosion of ground already poisoned with herbicides and other chemicals, which then are carried into the waterways. Even with the use of no-till and minimum-till technologies, an estimated half of the applied nitrogen fertilizer runs off into the Mississippi River and finally the dead zone of the Gulf of Mexico. Thus an enormous economic loss to farmers becomes an enormous ecological loss to everybody and to everybody's world.

VII – The industrial providers of single solutions assume that the agricultural structure of a country, a region, or a farm can be built piecemeal of disparate single parts, not necessarily or even probably fitting either the other parts or the farm or the local ecosystem, and yet ultimately resolving into a coherent, sensible, even a sustainable pattern by the disposition of the market. This obviously is nonsense.

VIII – A good or a sustainable farm cannot be made in this way. Its parts, even its industrial parts, can be made coherent and lasting only in obedience to the natural laws that order and sustain the local forest or prairie ecosystem. This is not an option. It is a necessity. By ignoring it, we have condemned our watersheds to continuous waste and pollution, and our cultures of husbandry to extinction.

IX – To hope to correct the consequent disorder, which is both human and natural, we have to begin by recognizing the fundamental incompatibility between industrial systems and natural systems, machines and creatures.

X – This recognition is not new. The problem was closely studied and made clear by such reputable people as J. Russell Smith, Albert Howard, and Aldo Leopold, whose publications were available and were ignored in the mid-twentieth century, when the all-out industrialization of farming got under way.

XI – I have now described the need for a farm bill that makes sense of and for agriculture—not the fiscal and political sense of agriculture, as in the customary five-year farm bills, but the ecological sense without which agricultural sense cannot be made, and without which agriculture cannot be made sustainable.

XII – The 50-Year Farm Bill, which has been in circulation now since 2009, is a proposal by The Land Institute in Salina, Kansas, with the concurrance of numerous allied groups and individuals. This bill addresses the most urgent problems of our dominant way of agriculture: soil erosion, toxic pollution of soil and water, loss of biodiversity, the destruction of farming communities and cultures. It addresses these problems by invoking Nature's primary law, in default of which her other laws are of no avail: Keep the ground covered, and keep it covered, by preference, with perennial plants.

XIII – At present, 80 percent of our farmable acreage is planted in annual crops, only 20 percent having the beneficent coverage of perennials. This, by the standard of any healthy ecosystem, is absurdly disproportionate. Annual plants are Nature's emergency medical service, covering wounds and scars to hold the land until the perennial cover is reestablished. By this rule, our present agriculture, giving 80 percent of our farmland to annuals, is in a state of emergency.

XIV – But you can't run a landscape, any more than you can run your life, indefinitely in a state of emergency. To live your life, to live in your place, you have got to bring about a settlement that does not involve you continuously in worry, loss, and grief. And so "A 50-Year Farm Bill" proposes a fifty-year schedule by which the present ratio of 80 percent annual to 20 percent perennial would be exactly reversed. The ratio then would be 20 percent annual to 80 percent perennial. And perhaps I need to say plainly here that the perennial crops would be forages and grains. Nobody at present is talking about the possibility of breeding and raising perennial table vegetables.

xv – By reversing the ratio of perennials to annuals, reducing annual plowing to one-fifth of the arable farm land, and making it possible to plow in any year only the least vulnerable land, soil erosion would be radically reduced. Chemical pollution also would be substantially reduced because perennials grown in mixtures such as grasses with legumes, as they already are in most pastures and many hayfields, are more self-sustaining and less chemical-dependent than annual monocultures.

xvi – This proposed great change would involve many smaller changes, all of which cannot be foreseen, let alone discussed in a short essay. I would like to enlarge upon just one of its implications.

xvii – The perennial plant cover we are talking about would be of several kinds: permanent pastures, pastures in rotation with row crops, perennial crops grown for hay or silage—and, starting perhaps within ten years, perennial grain crops grown in polycultures, which at times can, and probably should, be used for grazing.

XVIII – And so one of the most important results of the perennialization of agriculture would be the movement of farm
animals out of the wretched confinement factories where they
don't, and can never, belong, and back onto the pastures and
into the open air where they do belong.

XIX – Besides an immense kindness, this movement would be
a return to ecological health. It would transfer vast tonnages
of so-called "animal waste" from the water courses, where it
is a pollutant, to our food-producing acreage, where it is an
indispensable fertilizer. This, I hope, will also start us thinking
about the proper disposal of so-called "human waste."

XX – One of our great needs now is for human eaters to understand their eating as just one event within the fertility cycle,
the "Wheel of Life," by which, in the fullest state of health,
food is carried from the soil to the stomach, and then, as
so-called "waste," is carried back again to fertilize the soil. If
we keep faith with this cycle, we humans can continue to eat
indefinitely. Otherwise, we cannot.

XXI – The fertility cycle is a cycle entirely of living creatures
passing again and again through birth, growth, maturity,
death, and decay. Industrial technologies may shortcut the
cycle *for a while*, but such shortcuts also interrupt it, bringing
it, and us, presently into danger and eventually into disaster.

Speech for the Beard Foundation Food Conference
New York City, October 17–18, 2012

10

On Being Asked for "A Narrative for the Future"

I. [2013]

So far as I can see, the future has no narrative. The future does not exist until it has become the past. To a very limited extent, prediction has worked. The sun, so far, has set and risen as we have expected it to do. And the world, I suppose, will predictably end, but all of its predicted deadlines, so far, have been wrong.

The End of Something—history, the novel, Christianity,

the human race, the world—has long been an irresistible subject. Many of the things predicted to end have so far continued, evidently to the embarrassment of none of the predictors. The future has been equally, and relatedly, an irresistible subject. How can so many people of certified intelligence have written so many pages on a subject about which nobody knows anything? Perhaps we need a book—in case we don't already have one—on the end of the future.

None of us knows the future. Fairly predictably, we are going to be surprised by it. That is why "Take . . . no thought for the morrow . . ." is such excellent advice. Taking thought for the morrow is, fairly predictably, a waste of time.

I have noticed, for example, that most of the bad possibilities I have worried about have never happened. And so I have taken care to worry about all the bad possibilities I could think of, in order to keep them from happening. Some of my scientific friends will call this a superstition, but if I did not forestall all those calamities, who did? However, after so much good work, even I must concede that by taking thought for the morrow we have invested, and wasted, a lot of effort in preparing for morrows that never came. Also by taking thought for the morrow we repeatedly burden today with undoing the damage and waste of false expectations—and so delaying our confrontation with the actuality that today has brought.

The question, of course, will come: If we take no thought for the morrow, how will we be *prepared* for the morrow?

I am not an accredited interpreter of Scripture, but taking

thought for the morrow is a waste of time, I believe, because all we can do to prepare rightly for tomorrow is to do the right things today.

The passage continues: "for the morrow shall take thought for the things of itself. Sufficient unto the day is the evil thereof." The evil of the day, as we know, enters into it from the past. And so the first right thing we must do today is to take thought of our history. We must act daily as critics of history so as to prevent, so far as we can, the evils of yesterday from infecting today.

Another right thing we must do today is to appreciate the day itself and all that is good in it. This also is sound biblical advice, but good sense and good manners tell us the same. To fail to enjoy the good things that are enjoyable is impoverishing and ungrateful.

The one other right thing we must do today is to provide against want. Here the difference between "prediction" and "provision" is crucial. To predict is to foretell, as if we know what is going to happen. Prediction often applies to unprecedented events: human-caused climate change, the end of the world, etc. Prediction is "futurology." To provide, literally, is to see ahead. But in common usage it is to look ahead. Our ordinary, daily understanding seems to have accepted long ago that our capacity to see ahead is feeble. The sense of "provision" and "providing" comes from the past, and is informed by precedent.

Provision informs us that on a critical day—St. Patrick's

Day, or in a certain phase of the moon, or when the time has come and the ground is ready—the right thing to do is plant potatoes. We don't do this because we have predicted a bountiful harvest; history warns us against that. We plant potatoes because history informs us that hunger is possible, and we must do what we can to provide against it. We know from the past only that, if we plant potatoes today, the harvest *might* be bountiful, but we can't be sure, and so provision requires us to think today also of a diversity of food crops.

What we must *not* do in our efforts of provision is to waste or permanently destroy anything of value. History informs us that the things we waste or destroy today may be needed on the morrow. This obviously prohibits the "creative destruction" of the industrialists and industrial economists, who think that evil is permissible today for the sake of greater good tomorrow. There is no rational argument for compromise with soil erosion or toxic pollution.

For me—and most people are like me in this respect— "climate change" is an issue of faith; I must either trust or distrust the scientific experts who predict the future of the climate. I know from my experience, from the memories of my elders, from certain features of my home landscape, from reading history, that over the last 150 years or so the *weather* has changed and is changing. I know without doubt that to change is the nature of weather.

Just so, I know from as many reasons that the alleged causes of climate change—waste and pollution—are wrong. The right thing to do today, as always, is to stop, or start stopping, our habit of wasting and poisoning the good and beautiful things of the world, which once were called "divine gifts" and now are called "natural resources." I always suppose that experts may be wrong. But even if they are wrong about the alleged human causes of climate change, we have nothing to lose, and much to gain, by trusting these particular experts.

Even so, we are not dummies, and we can see that for all of us to stop, or start stopping, our waste and destruction today would be difficult. And so we chase our thoughts off into the morrow where we can resign ourselves to "the end of life as we know it" and come to rest, or start devising heroic methods and technologies for coping with a changed climate. The technologies will help, if not us, then the corporations that will sell them to us at a profit.

I have let the preceding paragraph rest for two days to see if I think it is fair. I think it is fair. As evidence, I will mention only that, while the theme of climate change grows ever more famous and fearful, land abuse is growing worse, noticed by almost nobody.

A steady stream of poisons is flowing from our croplands into the air and water. The land itself continues to flow or blow away, and in some places erosion is getting worse. High grain prices are now pushing soybeans and corn onto more and more sloping land, and "no-till" technology does not prevent erosion on continuously cropped grainfields. Industrial agriculture, moreover, is entirely dependent on burning the fossil fuels, the most notorious of the alleged causes of climate change.

Climate change, supposedly, is recent. It is apocalyptic, "big news," and the certified smart people all are talking about it, thinking about it, getting ready to deal with it in the future.

Land abuse, by contrast, is ancient as well as contemporary. There is nothing futurological about it. It has been happening a long time, it is still happening, and it is getting worse. Most people have not heard of it. Most people would not know it if they saw it.

The laws for conservation of land in use were set forth by Sir Albert Howard in the middle of the last century. They were nature's laws, he said, and he was right. Those laws are the basis of the 50-Year Farm Bill, which outlines a program of work that can be started now, which would help with climate change, but which needs to be done anyhow. Millions of environmentalists and wilderness preservers are dependably worried about climate change. But they are not conversant with nature's laws, they know and care nothing about land use, and they have never heard of Albert Howard or the 50-Year Farm Bill.

II. [2014]

If we understand that Nature can be an economic asset, a help and ally, to those who obey her laws, then we can see that she can help us now. There is work to do now that will make us her friends, and we will worry less about the future. We can begin backing out of the future into the present, where we are alive, where we belong. To the extent that we have moved out of the future, we also have moved out of "the environment" into the actual places where we actually are living.

If, on the contrary, we have our minds set in the future, where we are sure that climate change is going to play hell with the environment, we have entered into a convergence of abstractions that makes it difficult to think or do anything in particular. If we think the future damage of climate change to the environment is a big problem only solvable by a big solution, then thinking or doing something in particular becomes more difficult, perhaps impossible.

It is true that changes in governmental policy, if the changes were made according to the right principles, would have to be rated as big solutions. Such big solutions surely would help, and a number of times I have tramped the streets to promote them, but just as surely they would fail if not accompanied by small solutions. And here we come to the reassuring difference between changes in policy and changes in principle. The needed policy changes, though addressed to present evils, wait upon the future, and so are presently nonexistent. But changes in principle can be made now, by so few as just one of us. Changes in principle, carried into practice, are necessarily small changes made at home by one of us or a few of us. Innumerable small solutions emerge as the changed principles are adapted to unique lives in unique small places. Such small solutions do not wait upon the future. Insofar as they are possible now, exist now, are actual and exemplary now, they give hope. Hope, I concede, is for the future. Our nature seems to require us to hope that our life and the world's life will continue into the future. Even so, the future offers no validation of this hope. That validation is to be found only in the knowledge, the history, the good work, and the good examples that are now at hand.

There is in fact much at hand and in reach that is good, useful, encouraging, and full of promise, although we seem less and less inclined to attend to or value what is at hand. We are always ready to set aside our present life, even our present happiness, to peruse the menu of future exterminations. If the future is threatened by the present, which it undoubtedly is, then the present is more threatened, and often is annihilated, by the future. "Oh, oh, oh," cry the funerary experts, looking ahead through their black veils. "Life as we know it soon will end. If the governments don't stop us, we're going to destroy the world. The time is coming when we will have to do something to save the world. The time is coming when it will be too late to save the world. Oh, oh, oh." If that is the way our minds are afflicted, we and our world are dead already. The present is going by and we are not in it. Maybe when the present is past, we will enjoy sitting in dark rooms and looking at pictures of it, even as the present keeps arriving in our absence.

Or maybe we could give up saving the world and start to live savingly in it. If using less energy would be a good idea for the future, that is because it is a good idea. The government could enforce such a saving by rationing fuels, citing the many good reasons, as it did during World War II. If the government should do something so sensible, I would respect it much more than I do. But to wish for good sense from the government only displaces good sense into the future, where it is of no use to anybody and is soon overcome by prophesies of doom. On the contrary, so few as just one of us can save energy right now by self-control, careful thought, and remembering the lost virtue of frugality. Spending less, burning less, traveling less may be a relief. A cooler, slower life may make us happier, more present to ourselves, and to others who need us to be present. Because of such rewards, a large problem may be effectively addressed by the many small solutions that, after all, are necessary, no matter what the government might do. The government might even do the right thing at last by imitating the people.

In this essay and elsewhere, I have advocated for the 50–Year Farm Bill, another big solution I am doing my best to promote, but not because it will be good in or for the future.

I am for it because it is good now, according to present understanding of present needs. I know that it is good now because its principles are now satisfactorily practiced by many (though not nearly enough) farmers. Only the present good is good. It is the presence of good—good work, good thoughts, good acts, good places—by which we know that the present does not have to be a nightmare of the future. "The kingdom of heaven is at hand" because, if not at hand, it is nowhere.

Acknowledgments

The older I get the more clearly I see that no book, especially one such as this, should end without a giving of thanks. That is because no writer writes alone. A writer alone is unimaginable because impossible.

I thank my wife, Tanya Berry, whose generous attention to my work always involves her judgment, which is often better than mine—and often better than I at first think. (And I should add my thanks to our Royal Standard typewriter for standing up to the work for fifty-eight years, and for proof that machines do not have to wear out as soon as the warranty expires.)

I thank my children, Mary and Den, for being so rewardingly on my mind, and whose help with my thoughts is indispensable.

I thank my friends and brothers, John M. Berry, Jr., Wes Jackson, and Gene Logsdon, whose habits of thought are by now so familiar and present to me that they help me even when I don't ask, as they often have when I have asked.

I thank David Charlton, who knows what computers can do and how to make them do it, and who endures with exemplary patience my succession of next-to-final drafts.

I thank Troy Firth, Jason Rutledge, Jim Finley, and William Martin, who have generously made my essay, "A Forest Conversation," the subject of a forest conversation.

I thank Barth Johnson for most usefully helping me to worry about our rivers.

I thank Charlie Sing for the privilege of his conferences on agriculture and medicine.

I thank Robert B. Weeden, who has given me valuable help in several ways, and especially with the essay "Our Deserted Country."

I thank Jack Shoemaker of Counterpoint for his part of a literary collaboration, amounting exactly to friendship, of forty years.

I thank Julie Wrinn, copyeditor and reader, whose attention to my writing certainly has improved my own attention to it.

And I thank the editors of the following magazines in which several of these essays first were published in versions somewhat earlier: *Farming, The Progressive, The Christian Century, Harper's,* and *The Atlantic* (online).